CARE

BROOKE McALARY

CARE

THE RADICAL ART OF TAKING TIME.

ALLEN&UNWIN
SYDNEY · MELBOURNE · AUCKLAND · LONDON

To you,

who wants to change the world.

We can, and we must, proceed.

With care.

Brooke
xx

contents

prologue

Have you ever wondered where the days go once we live them?

When moments have turned into memories and stories and the slowly expanding growth rings of trees? Does time simply disintegrate, like ash on the wind? Does it live on in the smile lines around our eyes, the photos on our fridge, the lessons learnt and forgotten and relearnt? Can we harness time? Can we expand and fill it as we choose? Or is it fixed and rigid?

I think time is a wonderful, infuriating, gelatinous thing that constantly shifts and morphs. Some moments seem to stretch out far beyond the seconds they inhabit, while others escape through our fingers no matter how tightly we try to hold them. How else can we explain why some days slip swiftly by, while others are a slow-moving parade of moments that surely add up to more than twenty-four hours? How can some years leave us with hardly a memory and others leave everything transformed in their slow, boiling wake?

2020 was like that. One day everything felt normal, status quo in place (for better or worse) and, in the space of a few weeks, everything changed. It was the year time played tricks on us, when months seemed to last years while the year was somehow both the longest and shortest in memory.

2020 was the year our hearts broke. The year of kindness. The year of uncertainty. The year we craved each other. The year we hunkered down. The year of Zoom. The year of pause. The year of frustration. The year of hope. The year of sadness. The year we learnt the real value of a hug. It was also the year I discovered I cared too much. And the year I discovered I didn't care enough.

Care is love, compassion,
empathy, tenderness,
accuracy, attention,
responsibility, caution,
stewardship, maintenance,
repair, watchfulness
and assistance.

introduction

'Care'. As far as words go, it's
a relatively simple one, isn't it?

When we read it, maybe it conjures an image of a gardener tending their vegetable patch, a parent hugging a child, a nurse caring for a patient. Comforting, simple and wholesome. Dig a little deeper though, start to look at the multitude of ways we use the word 'care' in our lives, and suddenly it's quite a complicated little four-letter word, one that we have a complex relationship with.

Care is both something we can have (noun) and something we can do (verb). It can mean love, compassion, empathy, tenderness, accuracy, attention, responsibility, caution, stewardship, maintenance, repair, watchfulness and assistance. We care when we show up for people (*Let me care for you*) and withhold it to shut people out (*I don't care about that*). We harness it to fight for causes we believe in (*She cares passionately about this*) and deploy it as a defence mechanism to protect our vulnerabilities (*I couldn't care less what* he *thinks of me*). We can give it, deny it, guard it, offer it freely, mete it out frugally, remove it without warning and devote ourselves to it.

It's also a biological trait of every human being and sits at the evolutionary centre of our survival. Even Charles Darwin (yes, the father of the survival of the fittest theory) hypothesised that the species with the highest levels of sympathy and care built into their social structure would be the most likely to survive and thrive in a brutal world.

In spite of this, 'I don't care', or one of its variations, is a response many of us give in the course of a normal day. Not, I believe, because of a lack of decency in the modern world, but because our hard-wired need to care didn't evolve in today's world. A modern world that is full and noisy and busy and ripe with endless opportunities to care about virtually anything. Mere decades ago, our spheres of care were mostly limited to what was happening in our own communities or what we were shown on the nightly news. Now our devices feed us a steady diet of information, much of it simultaneously troubling and worthy of our attention. We hear terrible news; we see vitriol and prejudice writ large on our social-media timelines. We see our planet suffering, our fellow human beings divided along an increasing number of lines, while callousness and judgement and disunity dominate the conversation. Our ability to care is not limitless, our energy not infinite and, to put it plainly, we're exhausted. But because we're wired to, we try to care—even when it hurts. We care about the suffering of others, we care about the destruction of place, we care about injustice. And you know what? I think this capacity of ours to care is the superpower that will help us change the world.

Now, before you roll your eyes at the over-the-top grandiosity of that statement (and I'd understand if you did), let me add this—while yes, I believe that care is at the heart of changing the world, there are many, many ways of going about it and not all of them need to be big.

Like a lot of people, I spent the better part of 2020 caring hard. About the Covid pandemic, the climate crisis, racial injustice and social inequality. I gave almost all my attention, all my energy, all my care to reading and learning about these things, forming opinions about them, thinking about obstacles and solutions and actions at ungodly hours of the night. It seemed like every conversation, every interaction I had was seen through the lens of these enormous problems, and for a while, it felt good to care so much about them. It felt human. But over time, the lens became grimy with frustration and anger, and I found I could no longer see clearly. I think I got tired. So tired, that one morning, I couldn't get out of bed. I was physically, mentally and emotionally spent and I found myself numb to most of the things that had previously brought me joy. I stopped writing, I stopped gardening, I stopped reading, I stopped working altogether. I had no desire to connect, no desire to care. I retreated inward to escape the exhaustion. I didn't want to matter and I didn't want anything else to matter because, seemingly overnight, it had all begun to hurt—too much.

I realise now that I had slipped into the trap so many of us do and fallen headfirst into what I call Big Care—caring almost solely about those complex, global problems that dominate the headlines. At the time, though, it felt like I had suddenly stopped caring, and that was frightening.

I've since come to believe that we each have a personal spectrum of caring. It's not used to rank things as more or less worthy of our care, but to identify the different kinds of care that exist in our lives. On one end is Big Care: those expansive, global issues such as politics and environmental crises. On the other is self-care: our physical and mental health, mindfulness and self-talk. Both ends of the spectrum—as well as all the things in between—are valid and crucial, but I have a theory that much of what we experience as blind outrage or numbness or bone-deep emotional exhaustion in our modern lives actually comes from an imbalance in how we care.

When we focus solely on the big problems, we can become obsessive and overwhelmed, caught in a pattern of doom-scrolling and anger, and as a result lose sight of smaller, powerful, more accessible acts of care. Similarly, if we live exclusively in the realm of self-care, we risk becoming self-indulgent, sheltered and caught up in ever-shifting wellness trends without enjoying the wider benefits of community care. Living solely at either end of the spectrum can be exhausting and limiting in equal measure and will impact our health, relationships, self-esteem, families, communities and work.

Enter, Small Care. It can be found somewhere in the middle of the spectrum and is something I discovered in 2020, totally by accident, at a time when I felt completely wrung out by the world. I first noticed it in inconsequential actions like stopping to feel spring's first warm breeze on my face, cutting a bunch of flowers for my mum, smiling at a stranger, stargazing with my kids or picking up litter at the beach. Each tiny act was a choice to care, but to care in a way that left me feeling uplifted, buoyed somehow and part of something larger than myself. I didn't find these acts of care exhausting. I found them life-affirming.

Gradually, these small, outwardly trivial acts became a daily practice that helped me to heal, to reconnect, to find peace in a noisy world, to strengthen my relationships, to rebalance the scales in my own life, while also sending ripples of kindness into my relationships, my family, my community. By practising Small Care I was able to find my way back to a wobbly kind of equilibrium, and in doing so discovered just how powerful these tiny acts can be.

None of which is to say that Big Care is unimportant. Far from it, so please don't mistake any of this for cynicism or laziness. If we're going to fix the big issues, we need good people—people like you and me—to care about them and to care enough to work towards change. But we can't *only* care about these big, world-sized issues.

If we ignore our own health and wellbeing and the relationships and communities that weave together to make a life, then we will see the foundation of our personal world crumble. It's simply not possible to engage in long-term world-changing if we are sick, lonely, disconnected, without wonder or curiosity or kindness or joy. There's no point having the most loving, generous heart if you're too fatigued to use it and, my friend, let me tell you, the world needs your heart.

Typically, this might lead us into a discussion of the importance of self-care. And while I think self-care is a vital part of living well, I don't think it's the only part. Yes, it's a soothing, necessary balm for the scrapes and scars we acquire living in a hard-edged world and if that's what you need right now then know this: you are worthy of self-care and no, it isn't selfish.

But if you find yourself in a place where self-care feels stressful or inaccessible or a personal responsibility that is too much to bear, that's okay too. That's less a reflection of you and more a reflection on the present-day, capitalist version of self-care we're currently being sold.

To illustrate, let me share a story.

When I was a teenager, I used to wear a silver ring on my right thumb. It was a little too big, very shiny and stamped with the symbol for anarchy—a red paint-slash 'A' inside a circle. I bought it from a stall at a market in Sydney selling mass-produced crap, where you could find rip-off versions of pretty much anything you wanted—'Luis Vitton' bags, 'adihash' tracksuits, 'Pogo Ralph Laruen' T-shirts.

I bought that ring not because I was a budding anarchist (at fourteen years old I couldn't have explained to you what that meant) but because I'd seen someone else at school wearing one and thought it looked cool. I thought that by wearing one, I would look cool too. As a now late-thirty-something-year-old, the irony is not lost on me. The symbol of a stridently counter-cultural movement being mass-produced, stripped of its meaning and sold to a clueless teenager who really just wanted to fit in? It's funny, and a fairly common tale, because as long as there have been counter-cultural movements there has been the bastardisation of them. If there's even a whiff of profitability attached to these movements, there have been people trying to profit from them, while simultaneously diluting them—making them more palatable and infinitely more marketable.

Jazz music, hippies, hip-hop, punks, van-lifers, tiny houses, slow living: all counter-cultural movements, all with their roots in honest attempts to redefine freedom or success or joy or expression or community. All of them were first ignored by the mainstream, then openly derided, then grudgingly accepted and eventually even applauded, before the originators were shuffled aside, the Mad Men brought in and the question asked—how can we package this up and sell it back to the public in a neater, more lucrative way? It's in this shuffle that the guts and heart of these movements are often lost or adulterated beyond recognition, the essence of what made them good and real and attractive stripped away to fit in the mainstream.

Self-care has suffered the same fate. A movement that began with the desire of medical professionals to provide institutionalised patients some measure of independence by teaching them skills such as personal grooming and exercise (i.e. learning to *care* for them*selves*) has become a commodified shadow of its original form. After the term was coined by doctors in the 1950s, self-care was adopted by the civil rights movement in the United States in the late 1960s and became one of the key tenets of the Black Panther Party in the 1970s as they fought for equality in health care for Black communities, which are historically underserved in health care and social services.

when we connect we are caring

Self-care was rebooted by medical professionals in the early 2000s as PTSD diagnoses were on the rise in a post 9/11 world and offered as a complementary form of self-guided therapy for those suffering from work-related trauma. In today's world, self-care is still a technical term used by doctors to encourage us to care for ourselves in four key areas—our mental, emotional, psychological and spiritual health—by focusing on things such as nutrition, sleep, mindset, exercise and improving general wellbeing. In reality though, the term is used far more broadly and often for commercial ends. The global self-care industry has well and truly boomed, with an estimated value of nearly half a trillion dollars. When people talk about self-care today, it's more likely than not that they mean products and services—face masks, yoga retreats, meditation app subscriptions and home-delivered liver-cleansing regimes—rather than the intentional practice of taking care of their whole self. In fact, at least based on many of the millions of #selfcare social-media posts, it appears that to practise self-care (and presumably achieve wellness) we need to start by being affluent and *already well.*

If you've spent any time in the Instagram self-care/wellness sphere over the past few years, you've no doubt come across this quote from poet and activist Audre Lorde's 1988 book *A Burst of Light*: 'Caring for myself is not self-indulgence. It is self-preservation, and that is an act of political warfare.'

The modern self-care conversation seems to have focused more on the first half of this quote rather than the 'act of political warfare', hearing the words as a clarion call to guilt-free pampering, rather than to the necessary, self-driven, internal support required by people who are bone-tired from fighting for equality.

Now, I understand that we live in a capitalist society, but why does self-care suddenly require us to buy things in order to take part? And why are so many of those things making us feel a bit shit about ourselves at the same time? (Take time for you, girl. You deserve it. Here's a $39 sheet mask that will help you unwind after a tough week and will shrink those large pores. Win–win!)

There's no doubt that self-care, in its truest form, is vital to each of us. If we're exhausted or worn down or all cared out, it's important to give ourselves the opportunity to recharge, and taking time to care for yourself is a very powerful way of doing that. It's just that so much of what passes as self-care now is inaccessible or makes us feel like we're not good enough.

The kind of care I'm exploring in this book is not the Big kind, nor is it solely the self-focused kind. It's respectively smaller and more expansive than either of them. It's gentler, closer and more accessible. It's the yin to Big Care's yang, and the pepper to self-care's salt. I'm talking about care that is small, slow and sustainable but also surprisingly powerful.

This book, at its heart, is about the hundreds of acts of Small Care that are available to every one of us, every day, regardless of our circumstances, geography, income, physical or mental health, abilities or disabilities. It's about the many faces of care and why some of its most transformative effects come when we simply take a little time. When we connect, are kind, find awe in the world, spend time in nature, rediscover play, create, heal and even do nothing at all, we are caring.

I have a firm belief that by learning how to weave these acts into our daily lives, we will discover the key to unlocking the door between our close, personal lives and the world at large. And, by extension, discover how those small, personal acts of care can be acts of care for the world too.

Some of this might seem a bit much. Or perhaps you're thinking to yourself that, as nice as it sounds, none of it applies to you. Your life is too busy, too complex, too full to take the time for anything other than keeping your head above water, finding work, buying groceries or paying rent. These are all real concerns, of course, and all worth your attention, but I also think that none of them are permanent obstacles to learning how to take a little time for a little care.

Your time-bending toolkit

In my second book, *Slow*, I dug deep into the how and, more importantly, the why of slowing down in your day-to-day life. Somewhat unintentionally, this book has been written as a companion—not because you need to read both, but because both *Slow* and this book explore time: how to create more of it, how to make the most of it, how to lengthen it out so that a minute spent adds up to far more than 60 seconds. Before we head into the heart and guts of care, I would like to hand you some tools that you can use as we go exploring. Readers of *Slow* might recognise some of these ideas, but even so I'd encourage you to pick them up one at a time, hold them in your hands and ask how they might help you.

These tools aren't designed for constant use, but rather to be put to work and put back down again as needed. Like all tools, they'll make your job easier, doing some of the hard work for you, but also like all tools, they only work if you actually use them.

TOOL #1: BENDING TIME

Time is a shape-shifter. When we're kids it moves slowly, as we watch the clock's hands inch towards the last bell of the school day, or as we wait impatiently for Christmas morning to arrive. The more we want something to hurry up, the slower it comes, until of course it does come and then, in a flurry of excitement, it's gone and the swampy feel of a Monday morning or the happy-sad feeling of Boxing Day meets us on the other side.

Somewhere between Christmas morning and becoming a grown-up, time changes. We find ourselves bewildered at the swift stream of it, marking every December with a familiar pronouncement like, 'This year has flown!' or 'Every year gets faster!'

Why does this happen? Does time automatically speed up when we graduate high school? Or when we get our first job? The spiral of years turns and turns, tighter and tighter, until we feel like we're going up and down in the one spot.

As poetically depressing as that sounds, scientists believe that there are real reasons why we experience time differently as we grow up, and it's not because clocks run faster the older we get.

One theory suggests that during the slow-moving years of childhood, our brains are constantly processing new information. New words, skills, joys, pains, triumphs, games and sounds. Our brains need to pay attention to these new experiences because we're learning about ourselves and the world through our exposure to them. There is so much to process and so many new memories being created.

As we get older, and the rate at which we learn new things or have new experiences tends to drop steeply, our brains become very efficient at skipping over those tasks we do repeatedly. As we cook the same foods, walk the dog on the same trails, follow the same routines every morning, catch the same bus, make the same small talk, visit the same places, look at the same views out the same windows, our brains decide that these repeated experiences aren't really worth remembering. This means we forget them, remembering less of our days and weeks and months, which, in turn, speeds up our perception of time and its passing. This is why specific moments in a day might feel slow as we grind through them, but when we look back on the week, the month or even the year, it feels like time has flown by. What's more, proportionally speaking

Every day,
every moment,
is ripe for noticing,
for taking and
spending well.

at least, a child who has lived less time than an adult will experience each hour as a bigger slice of the time pie; an adult who has lived double, triple, ten times as many years will have a totally different perspective on time.

This is where your Time-bending tool comes in. David Eagleman is a neuroscientist from Stanford University who has spent many years studying time perception and brain plasticity. His research has shown that one of the best ways to slow down time is to do something new, saying, 'The more detailed the memory, the longer the moments seem to last.' But even the tiniest of shifts to your normal routine can work. You might wear a new lipstick or listen to a new podcast, perhaps you try sitting in a different train carriage or take notes by hand rather than on your laptop. You could spend a moment noticing a new detail every day—a tree you've never really seen, the way the lace on your shirt is so intricately woven, how newsprint is made up of tiny coloured dots or the way the sun is backlighting the hair of the stranger in front of you, making it look like gold—it doesn't really matter, so long as it's new and different from your norm. Doing this shocks our brain into paying attention again, recording our experiences, filling our mind with new memories. Stretching our perception of time and making it *more.*

This tool is something we all possess, it's just waiting for its chance to come out, to bend and stretch time, maybe for the first time since you were a child. We may not be able to stop every second ticking by, spooling out, but we can make some of them *more.* We can take that time and spend it well and give ourselves more of this resource we have such a changeable relationship with. When we turn off autopilot, when we stop and pay attention, we gift ourselves more time. More new experiences to look back on, more opportunities for wonder and magic and beauty and joy at the realisation that every day, every moment, is ripe for noticing, for taking and spending well.

TOOL #2: THE NOT-KNOWING

Throughout this book you'll notice I ask a lot of questions. Sometimes they're rhetorical, but mostly they offer an opportunity for you to provide the answer. I'm simply asking because I'm curious. I wrote this book because I want to know what the ripple effects of taking time for Small Care might look like and how we can use simple, accessible ideas to change the world. Part of me wishes I had the answers before I began, but another, larger part enjoys the not-knowing.

This wasn't always the case. As a kid, and even into adulthood, I thought I avoided asking questions because I didn't want to seem impolite or nosy. It wasn't until I was older that I realised there was another reason I didn't ask questions, and it was far more detrimental—I was loath to show that I didn't already know the answer. I didn't want to look stupid or ignorant, so I stayed silent and, ironically, remained more ignorant than I would have been had I simply asked questions.

I've since learnt that there is freedom in admitting that we don't have all the answers, and an even greater liberation in knowing that we don't need them. We don't have to carry certainty around like a shield and will be better equipped with a sense of curiosity and by understanding that not-knowing is human. Admitting to our not-knowing opens up channels for learning, for growth and for connection we couldn't find otherwise.

Not-knowing is curiosity, it's experimentation, it's *What if?* and *Why not?* and *Let's see what's around this corner.* It might even help to picture it as a magnifying glass you keep in your back pocket. When you find yourself unsure, instead of making assumptions or pretending you already know the answer, pull out this tool and take a minute to look deeper. Learn to ask questions. Use what you discover to open your mind to new and different possibilities, to the likelihood that your point of view is only one of many.

You can also use this tool to help you see the ideas and suggestions in this book through a lens of experimentation, to ask yourself, *What might happen if . . . ?* and then try it, open to the outcome, whatever it might be. The beauty of viewing new, foreign or challenging ideas through this lens of experimentation is that you simultaneously open yourself up to the not-knowing while letting go of the need to achieve a certain result. You become receptive to trying new things and keep yourself open to all possibilities.

The magnifying glass may just help you look closer, while also broadening your understanding of the world.

~~~~~~~~~~

TOOL #3: UNPLUG

This book isn't about demonising technology. In fact, I believe tech has a vital role to play in our world, but that doesn't mean allowing it to take up inordinate amounts of space in our lives.

Did you know that the average smartphone user spends around three hours and fifteen minutes on their phone every day? This adds up to more than twenty-two hours a week—nearly an entire day, every week, spent on our phones. Given that many people feel the reason they don't do things like spend more time with family or read a book or go for a walk in nature is because they don't actually have the time to spend, I think it's fair to ask the question: what would happen if we reduced our phone time?

Here's something that might help spark a fire in your belly. Did you know that Bill Gates' three children weren't allowed to own a smartphone until they turned fourteen? Or that some Silicon Valley tech executives send their kids to exclusive private schools where the use of technology such as tablets, computers and other screens is heavily limited, if not uniformly banned, due to their negative impact on learning outcomes? And my favourite: did you know that Steve Jobs refused to let his children use iPads when they were young?

In 2010, not long after the release of the first iPad, New York University professor Adam Alter asked Jobs whether his kids were enjoying the new device, to which Jobs responded, 'Actually we don't allow the iPad in the home. We think it's too dangerous for them in effect.'

Huh. Interesting.

We all know that the apps and games we install on our devices are designed to get us hooked but if, like me, you've ever felt that you're not acting entirely of your own volition when your phone is in hand, you're not wrong. When we unlock our phone and see a little red notification dot, or when we hear the ping of a new message or email, our brains release a mini hit of dopamine— a neurotransmitter that helps us feel pleasure, satisfaction and motivation—which then conditions us to see this behaviour as positive, encouraging us to do more of it. Essentially these pings, notifications and likes are creating an addictive, positive-feedback loop that becomes increasingly difficult to break. You're not just battling your own willpower every time you feel drawn to pick up your phone, you're also battling an entire industry of very smart people, whose job it is to get and keep you checking and scrolling and tapping.

I'm not talking about tossing your iPhone away (I'm also not *not* saying that could be a good idea), but instead want to encourage you to use the Unplug tool whenever you feel you need to even out the balance a little.

I could offer you all kinds of hacks and tips to help reduce your screen time, but the most effective way I've learnt to unplug is to simply notice more. I start by noticing how my phone and all the noise and information it brings into my life makes me feel. Notice how I feel if I leave it on the hallway table rather than keeping it in my pocket. Notice my reactions when I switch it off for an entire day over the weekend. Notice how my mornings unfold if I don't check my emails or the news headlines before 9 am. Notice what happens when I delete Instagram for a month.

Then I notice other things, things in my life that aren't on a screen—both big and small. I notice the people and places I love, the work I enjoy, the smell of fresh rain on dirt, holding hands with my kids, reading a great book, going for a hike, camping somewhere with no wi-fi, laughing with friends. I notice how I feel when these things fill my time. I notice the lightness of heart, the satisfaction of tired muscles, the quiet contentment in a moment of silence.

The real hack is to build a life that is so full of the tangible things that matter, that even when you do pick up your phone, you'll know there is so much goodness waiting for you outside your screen that the lure of scrolling through those dopamine-dosing apps isn't nearly as strong as it used to be and you can put your phone down again. You'll realise that life outside the screen is too juicy and wonderful to waste.

~~~~~~~~~

TOOL #4: YOUR INNER REBEL

Everyone has one. That version of yourself that lives inside (sometimes so deep inside as to seem non-existent) that worries less about the shoulds of the world and more about the feel of things. The version who is happy to dance to their own unique rhythm, confident that they're living in alignment with their personal values.

It's not easy to tap into this inner rebel when we're surrounded by expectations to fulfil, ladders to climb and masks of success to wear.

But this version of you knows things. They know what fills you with joy. They know the specific place in your belly that warms when you find yourself in a state of rightness. They know your deepest held desires and what you'd do with an entirely free day if given the chance. They know where you're happiest, when you feel the most supported, which rituals fill your heart with gladness. They're not interested in tick-boxes or ladders or shoulds. They are your inner rebel and they love raising eyebrows.

Before you can use this tool, you first need to spend a little time looking for your inner rebel. Maybe paint a picture in your mind of where they live, how they move through their days, what they think of all the expectations you carry. Mine, for example, lives in an off-grid cabin in the bush somewhere up north. She swims in the dam every morning, with yabbies and ducks for company. She lets her hair dry loose and messy in the breeze and doesn't own a phone. Or a TV. She listens to music all the time, mostly turned up loud, and sings with no self-consciousness. She gardens and shares what she can with friends and neighbours. She laughs a lot. Hugs trees. Picks up rubbish from the beach. She's a lot like me on the days I'm not so weighed down by the world, and I often turn to her when I'm looking for that gut-check guidance I need. When there's a decision to make, she will often point me down the road less travelled.

I don't know how she makes money, or whether she lives in her cabin alone, or if she has a car. None of these details matter because she's not really a separate person, and by getting to know her I'm just exploring another facet of myself. The hippie-punk-rock-granny version, who has answers, who knows my heart. She's my anti-establishment mirror image.

Once you have a blurry image of your own inner rebel, imagine putting a photo of them in your back pocket and keeping it tucked in there (alongside your magnifying glass), bringing it out any time you're feeling that pull to stray from the well-worn path but are unsure how to do it. Your inner rebel might remind you that wisdom is hard-won, and often found on the road less travelled.

As I said, feel free to pick these tools up as needed and put them back down again when you're done. No one's asking you to spend all day, every day, trying new things, or to infuriate your friends by constantly asking, 'Why?', to live without your phone forever or to relocate to the bush, living off-grid with your inner rebel. But each of these tools offers a different way to approach the ideas in this book, and it's my hope that by picking them up, and using them as needed, you'll find many different ways to care.

Before we begin

Where we go in the following chapters might surprise you. I know that it surprised me. While connection, kindness and healing (Chapters 1, 2 and 9) seem like straightforward ways to show care, what about seeking awe in the world? Or spending time in nature? Making something, playing, moving our bodies or practising idleness? These aren't typical examples of what we consider care.

Honestly, that's the whole point. I want to change the conversation around care, open it up to include more than Big Care, more than self-care, more than the types of caring that we associate with parents and nurses and teachers and conservationists. I want to ask the question: What would happen if we all took a little time to practise Small Care?

I think the radical part is two-fold. First, to rethink care completely, to simplify it and make it a choice we can each make, every day. The second radical part is what happens when we do.

How the benefits of each of the types of care we're about to explore not only impact us positively, but also affect the people we know and love, the work we do, the towns and suburbs and cities we live in, the communities we belong to. The ripples of care have far greater range than we might think at first—certainly far greater than I thought possible when I started writing this book. And the thing I want you to know before we start is that everything we need to begin is within us already: our ability to bend time, our innate curiosity, our capacity to look up and search.

On a practical note, at the end of every chapter, you'll find a list of real-world suggestions to help you experiment with different types of care. I've tried to be as mindful as possible of the different circumstances each of you might be in, the time we do or don't have, the access or capability or finances we may or may not possess at any given moment, and I am fairly confident there will be something on each of the lists for everyone. Some of these ideas will appeal to you, some of them won't; others might be new or scary or so tiny as to feel absurd. You don't have to do them all. Each list is merely a starting point for you to explore what care looks like for you.

Connection. Kindness. Awe. Nature. Making. Movement. Play. Rest. Healing.

These are the nine core ideas of this book. The nine seeds you can plant within yourself and that will, over time and with a little care, grow into plants that bring joy and beauty and wonder to your life. Plants that will flower and fruit and produce seeds of their own, which will fall onto nearby soil, creating a ramshackle patchwork of plants that radiates out from you, gradually and repeatedly changing the world.

With that in mind, let's get into it, shall we?

Connection. Kindness.
Awe. Nature. Making.
Movement. Play.
Rest. Healing.

These are the nine core
ideas of this book.

CHAPTER 1

connection

Draw a red thread

from me, to you—

straight as an arrow.

Draw a red thread

from you, to a stranger,

in an unseen town

in an unseen country

under an unseen sky.

Pull that red thread,

see how it tightens

how it draws us closer

how it ties our hearts together.

Consider the sad release when it's cut

and the terrifying, dizzy joy

when we spool out another red thread

in hope, in trust, in connection—

straight as an arrow.

Have you ever played Six Degrees of Kevin Bacon?

It's a game that operates on the theory that any actor in Hollywood can be connected to Kevin Bacon in six steps or less. If it sounds silly, you're right—it is, but it's also fun. Let's play a quick round, you'll see why in a minute.

At the risk of sounding morbid, the *Hunger Games* movies are my go-to comfort-watch (don't judge me), so let's take one of its stars, Elizabeth Banks, to start. Banks played Effie Trinket in all four movies, which also starred Julianne Moore as Alma Coin. Moore appeared in the 2011 film *Crazy Stupid Love* alongside none other than Mr Kevin Bacon. So, Elizabeth Banks has a Bacon Number of two, and Julianne Moore has the highest possible number of one, because she's worked directly with Kevin Bacon himself.

Make sense? Sort of? Okay.

Let's look at another *Hunger Games* star—Jennifer Lawrence. This is a simple one because Lawrence played Mystique in the 2011 film *X-Men: First Class,* which also starred our boy Kevin. So, Jennifer Lawrence has an Oscar, three Golden Globes and a Bacon Number of one.

Finally, let's look at British actress, radical inclusivity activist and all-round good egg Jameela Jamil. Aside from appearing in Mike Schur's excellent show *The Good Place,* Jamil was in the 2019 film *How to Build a Girl,* alongside Paddy Considine. He appeared in the 1999 teen comedy-drama *A Room for Romeo Brass* with the legendary Bob Hoskins, who will forever be Smee from *Hook* to me and who also voiced the role of Boris Goosinoff, a snow goose in the 1995 animated film *Balto,* which, yes, starred the one and only Kevin Bacon. Phew. This means Jamil has a Bacon Number of three—

which was kind of difficult to find out. Turns out Mr Bacon is prolific and very well connected. (Okay. I'm done now.)

Yes, it's fun if you like movies and completely useless trivia like me, but it's also an unscientific way of establishing what most of us already know on some level: we live in a hyper-connected world. Just like Six Degrees of Kevin Bacon, we're only a few clicks away from nearly any person or piece of information we could possibly want to access and in some ways that makes the world feel much smaller and closer.

What a time to be alive, right?

Right!

Except.

Except that although we may be more connected than ever, we're also lonelier than ever.

This paradox was never so evident as during our Covid lockdowns. In what can only be described as the Zoom Boom, technology became the lifeline many of us clung to when we realised just how important human connection is. There's little doubt that video calls or chatting on the phone can help to alleviate some of the feelings of loneliness that prolonged isolation can deliver, but ongoing research appears to show that it's not enough to keep loneliness at bay.

In 2018, research conducted by Swinburne University found that one in every four Australians regularly experienced feelings of loneliness. Social distancing and various lockdowns as a result of the Covid pandemic appear to have added significantly to that statistic, with the first wave of data from an ongoing loneliness study, also conducted by Swinburne University, showing that as many as one in every two Australians is now regularly experiencing loneliness. It's also been revealed that younger people (aged 18–25), those with mental health issues and those living in single-person households are among the most severely impacted.

Next time you find yourself walking down the street or sitting on a train, take a moment to use your Unplug tool by looking up and noticing the people near you. Consider them, as they take up space in the world, as they move through their days. Approximately every second one of them has felt lonely this week, and every fourth person has spent nearly half their week feeling lonely. Are you one of them? Are your kids, friends, parents or neighbours?

I was 37 when I admitted to myself that I was crushingly lonely. I was two books deep into my writing career and 300 episodes into hosting a podcast that allowed me to regularly have interesting and honest conversations with a wide variety of people. I had strong, supportive relationships with my husband Ben, my kids, sisters and parents. I had a Bacon Number of four for goodness' sake. (I interviewed Sheri Salata in 2019, Sheri Salata was Executive Producer of the final five seasons of *Oprah*, Oprah appeared in *Selma* with Cuba Gooding Jr, and Cuba Gooding Jr starred in *A Few Good Men* with Kevin Bacon). And I was very, very lonely.

After travelling a lot and moving away from where I'd grown up, many of my friends lived far away from me and, although I felt seen and supported and understood when I was near them, once I moved out of their orbit I'd drift back into loneliness. The Instagram messages or emails or texts never filled the friend-shaped holes that were left. Not quite.

As someone who has taken every personality test known to humankind and who consistently measures at around 97 per cent introverted, I'd tried to convince myself that the friends I did have were enough, and I really didn't need to have any of them nearby. I'd also convinced myself that I didn't really want my friends in close proximity because I valued my alone time and therefore couldn't really complain about being lonely. However, there is a very big difference between being alone and being lonely.

The truth was that I hadn't prioritised friendship. I allowed myself to think that digital connection—a Facebook 'Happy Birthday', a belated response to a text, an Instagram message when I found myself thinking about them—was enough. I allowed myself to think I was self-sufficient when in fact I was isolated and left wanting. Really, I was afraid of reaching out and coming back empty-handed, so I stayed lonely.

That meant I had no one to call when I had a rough day. No one to have coffee and download with. No one at the school gate in the afternoon who saw through the persona I put on when my anxiety was biting hard. And I tried for a long time to convince myself that I was okay with that. More than okay, that being an introvert and someone who valued a 'slow life' actually required that of me.

It wasn't until I met a work acquaintance for a coffee one day and our conversation drifted to her recent run of shockingly bad Tinder dates and the vacuousness of online dating that I blurted out how lonely I was. I was mortified. Tinder-chat aside, this was a work meeting. I'd only met her once before—why did I think she'd care?

As I sat with that discomfort for a moment, allowing the shame and guilt and embarrassment to wash over me, I realised that not only did she seem unfazed, but that my admission had actually kickstarted a new conversation about loneliness. One where she shared her own desire for real connection and the struggle to find it in a world of shitty Tinder dates and shallow social-media interactions.

Not long after that conversation, my family and I moved to a completely new area, to a small town where we knew no one and had to start our community connections from scratch. Within a couple of months, I could no longer convince myself I was okay being self-contained and self-sufficient. I was sad and lonely and needed to connect.

Over several months I began experimenting with different approaches, curious to see what would happen if I opened up a little more, shifting myself ever so slightly into the discomfort zone. I first began spending time working in our local coffee shop rather than always working from home (this was pre-Covid, obviously). While there was a thrill of recognition when I was on a first-name basis with the people who worked there, I also recognised something else. Even on the days I didn't chat to anyone, my energy was higher. Simply being around other people, interacting in the simplest of ways, felt good. I'd been starving myself of this energy and hadn't realised.

Over time (and not much of it—just a few weeks), I felt buoyed to try new things. I started volunteering at the kids' school—something I'd been curious about but too nervous to do. I got in touch with a local arts collective to see if there were any co-working spaces I could use. I signed up for a yoga class and aikido lessons in our local area and prioritised attending them. I joined a couple of community projects and started to see how I might be able to help. I began being more open in conversations with friends and strangers alike, and less concerned with fitting in.

What began as an experiment in being around people more frequently had quite quickly become the catalyst for bringing up the floor on the deepest parts of my loneliness. I realised that I'd bought wholeheartedly into one specific idea of what constitutes friendship and spent years believing that I was somehow deficient because I didn't have it. No 'tribe' of girlfriends who frequently appeared on each other's social-media accounts. No ride-or-dies, no Galentine's Day posts. I was so focused on that one version of friendship I completely missed all the other types of connection the world has to offer and the benefits they hold. I didn't need to go out and make five new best friends, maybe I just needed to learn how to connect more deeply with the people already in my life. Maybe I needed to look up and realise that the world is full of opportunities to connect and not all of them are hard, even for an introvert. Maybe I needed to use the time I already spent with people more mindfully.

Clearly community offers us an antidote to loneliness, but what other reasons are there to connect? Why else is human-to-human connection important?

How did we get so distant?

We have evolved over hundreds of thousands of years to value connection and thrive when it's in place. We are not loners by nature—historically depending on other members of our tribe or village for help to find food, shelter, love and a sense of belonging— and yet our hyper-connected, tech-heavy, convenience-driven society has removed so much of the face-to-face interaction we have always relied on, leaving many of us socially isolated without necessarily understanding where our sense of disconnection comes from.

Answers to the question of why we are so much lonelier vary— some researchers have found that increased use of technology and social media is the problem, particularly in younger people, while others are looking at the rise of individualism in society, the pace of modern life, and how our towns and cities now offer little opportunity for community connection or space to congregate. I suppose we now have to add to this the very real possibility that, because of Covid, people may also be afraid to connect face-to-face. The pandemic gave us a new kind of fear that has driven us to use tech more, in place of the in-person interactions we used to have. Things like contactless delivery and apps that allow us to order and pay for our coffee remotely cut out even the simplest of interpersonal interactions and are stripping us of the pleasure of day-to-day human contact.

The more we connect with people, the better we feel about ourselves »› the more we empathise with and trust others, the more others open up and trust us »› the more we value that trust, the more we open up and trust others.

Whatever the cause, disconnection is impacting us in myriad ways—not only to the detriment of our physical and mental health, but also our relationships, communities, workplaces and homes. In other words, the very societies we live in are being crippled by disconnection and loneliness.

In a 2017 meta-analysis of dozens of studies on loneliness, Julianne Holt-Lunstad and a team of researchers at Brigham Young University found that regularly feeling lonely or isolated has the equivalent effect of smoking approximately fifteen cigarettes a day, and that those of us who experience prolonged or frequent feelings of loneliness are nearly 50 per cent more likely to die prematurely. High blood pressure, cardiovascular disease, cognitive decline and depression are some of the conditions affected by loneliness that can contribute to mortality.

While it might be easy to cast this as a personal, albeit common, problem, the truth is that loneliness is a massive public health issue that could be costing us up to $60 billion annually in health care and lost productivity. This is not a personal problem, it's an everyone problem.

Loneliness might feel like a shameful secret you're embarrassed to admit in a world where it feels like everyone else is constantly surrounded by a tight-knit group of supportive mates—and you might feel like you're losing the real-life version of Six Degrees of Kevin Bacon—but let me assure you, you're not alone in feeling lonely.

Finding connection

Connecting with other people more frequently doesn't only benefit us by reducing levels of loneliness either—the benefits of increasing our interaction with other humans are surprisingly far-reaching and include:

- strengthened immune system
- reduced levels of inflammation
- faster recovery from illness and disease
- reduction in the effects of stress
- improved heart health
- improved gut function
- improved insulin regulation
- prolonged life expectancy
- lower rates of anxiety and depression
- higher self-esteem
- higher levels of resilience
- higher levels of humility
- increased self-confidence
- reduced perfectionist tendencies
- increased empathy
- greater sense of cooperation and trust.

In what is a beautiful, positive feedback loop, the more we connect with people, the better we feel about ourselves; the more we empathise with and trust others, the more others open up and trust us; the more we value that trust, the more we open up and trust others. It's a wellbeing win–win–win—socially, emotionally and physically.

Digital vs analog: the connection conundrum

We live in a digital world, or so the conventional wisdom goes. Many of us work digitally, we socialise digitally, we bank digitally (what is money at this point other than numbers in our banking app?), we're entertained and titillated and informed digitally. So many of the inputs to our lives and so many of the outputs of our energies are digital: so yes, by that definition, we live in a digital world.

But we are not digital creatures. Human beings cannot speak digital language. We aren't Neo from *The Matrix*. We do not understand the millions of ones and zeroes that allow us to stream The Beach Boys' 'God Only Knows' on Spotify. If we were to view the data that adds up to an ultra-high-resolution, digitised image of the *Mona Lisa*, we would only see incomprehensible digits in their millions, maybe even billions. No cascading melodies or plays of light.

There is beauty and creativity in the digital, no doubt, but it will remain a mystery to us until it is translated into a language we understand.

On the other hand, we have analog, which has two quite different meanings. The first is related to technology, where analog refers to devices in which information is represented by variable physical qualities as opposed to the fixed binary language of digital. So, a vinyl record is an analog technology because the sounds that make up music are created when the needle moves through tiny grooves on the surface of the record and vibrates. An mp3, meanwhile, is a digital technology because the song has been recorded, translated and encoded into a collection of 'bits' that are, at their core, a series of ones and zeroes that add up to a recording.

The second definition of analog refers to a person or thing that may be comparable or similar to another. An orphaned joey will snuggle into a knitted pouch as an analog to its mother's. Comparable, similar, but not the same.

Take a birthday message, sent to a friend. You could hand-write the message on a card and mail it to them. If you did, the note inside would be analog, not digital, because it's created in a tangible, physical way and when they open the card and read your message, the only translation that happens is between words and thoughts.

Alternatively, you could send the same message via text using your phone. As you type those words, the phone translates them into the ones and zeroes of digital information. Hundreds of them. They are then sent over the network as data to your friend's phone, where the message is re-translated into pixels that form letters, thereby allowing your friend to read their birthday message on their phone.

That's one side of the analog coin, so to speak.

The other side is that your text is an analog for an actual birthday card. Similar or comparable but not the same.

And I have to wonder—what's being lost in translation here? Undoubtedly, it's lovely to be thought of and contacted—no matter the format—but is the impact the same?

Receiving a handwritten note tends to stick with us a lot longer than a text or an email. I still have a small stack of notes from Ben that he wrote to me back in the early 2000s. In the years since, I'm sure he's written some equally lovely texts, but I don't treasure them in the same way. I've never printed out an email and lovingly added it to a stack of similar printouts tied with a blue ribbon.

It strikes me that in our digital world we not only need to create analog translations of information in order to understand it, but we've also surrounded ourselves with digital analogs for other things.

Social networks are an analog for in-person connection and community just as digital music is an analog for live music, and streamed movies are an analog for going to the cinema. Porn is an analog for sex or physical intimacy or our own personal fantasies; text messages are an analog for phone calls or letters.

We are surrounded by stand-ins and knock-offs and digital technologies that claim to be just as good, if not better than the analogs of old. I can't help but wonder—are they? What are we missing out on when we take the digital route every time?

A few years ago, author and computer science professor Cal Newport invited readers of his blog to join him in a month-long experiment, where he encouraged them to take a 31-day break from all 'optional technologies'. This included things like reading the news online and using social-media platforms such as Facebook, Twitter and Instagram. The idea was for participants to remove these inputs from their lives for a month after which they could 'rebuild their digital lives starting from a blank slate—only allowing back in technologies for which they could provide a compelling motivation'.

Newport was surprised when more than 1600 readers decided to join the experiment, and even more surprised when the results began rolling in. Not only did the participants enjoy stepping back from their daily habits of online news consumption and social-media scrolling, but they also 'often overhauled their free time in massively positive ways'. From reading more to learning to become a better listener, picking up previously forgotten hobbies such as chess, to finally finishing the novel manuscript that had been languishing in a drawer for years, participants discovered just how much time optional technologies had been costing them.

Even more fascinating to me was Newport's discovery that most people weren't just replacing mindless social-media scrolling with unrelated activities. He writes that 'in many cases, they were instead finding improved sources of the benefits that drew them to social media in the first place', and in that discovery are implications for our digital/analog conundrum.

For example, people who appreciated the entertainment value of social media often found themselves picking up analog creative hobbies such as painting or reading that gave them an even deeper sense of entertainment, while many who used social media to keep in touch with friends and family found that they spent those regained hours on things like phone calls or meeting in person. One participant who previously spent hours a week scrolling news websites in an effort to stay informed replaced that digital habit with a subscription to a physical newspaper and found that he was still just as informed as before 'without getting caught up in the minute-to-minute clickbait headlines and sensationalism that is so typical of online news'. Newport coined the term 'analog social media' to describe these real-world activities that seem to deliver heartier doses of the very benefits social media promises us: connection, like-minded people, deeper relationships, communities and shared interests.

Tech connection

When it comes to human connection, tech has its benefits. We saw this during our various Covid lockdowns, when all kinds of communication apps—FaceTime and House Party and Instagram— formed the backbone of our social and working lives. And while you'd understand the huge spike in Zoom calls for work, weekend Zoom calls also increased by more than 2000 per cent during lockdown. I've never loved communicating over video call, as I find it stilted and exhaustingly surface-level, but I've never been so grateful for the technology as I was during lockdown—and a positive side effect of this increased tech use was that it demonstrated a new kind of working behaviour. Suddenly it became clear that people living outside major cities, people living with a disability, people with young children or medically complex needs or mental health issues could all participate in the workforce in ways they might not previously have been able to because, suddenly, the old excuses no longer held. It became clear that many of us didn't need to commute into the city every day, we didn't need to take flights around the country or across the globe every year, we didn't need to work the traditional hours in the traditional office to be productive and efficient and good at our jobs. The technology we have at our disposal makes the new world, of more flexible hours, remote working and less time commuting, available to many of us.

Tech offers us accessibility, inclusivity and the ability to connect, but it shouldn't be a replacement for human connection. If we all work from home, socialise from home, order meals from home, shop from home and are entertained at home, we could say we're ticking all the important boxes in living well, but without connection, without face-to-face human interaction, we're missing out on a huge chunk of what life has to offer.

I believe that tech should be a tool—one we use for a specific purpose—to create or connect or build something. Then it should be put down as we move on to other things. Tech can be the hammer and the saw and the screwdriver we use to build walls or windows or roofs, but tech shouldn't be the house we live in.

To strike some kind of balance between analog and digital, we need to try new things, so the rest of this chapter will focus on different ways to get more analog in how you connect with people. Strangers, partners, neighbours, colleagues, fellow commuters or bar flies, it doesn't matter because we're ultimately wired for connection. Some of the ideas might feel uncomfortable or foreign, but I'd encourage you to keep an open mind, that perhaps the discomfort you feel is less about the experiments themselves and more about how far removed we've become from personal interaction. No one's here to force you to reconcile with estranged family members or send a letter to your high-school bully; these experiments are simply about recognising that we are surrounded by other human beings and that connecting with them in a meaningful way has ripple effects that will reach further than you might imagine.

Being vulnerable

Vulnerability is the structural foundation of connection. Without it we can't deepen our relationships and we can't build trust. Despite that, vulnerability is often seen as weakness. In fact, I'd say that before Brené Brown stormed into our hearts and minds with her 2010 TED talk and the rallying cry that vulnerability is a superpower, I'd only ever really thought of vulnerability in a negative context. The castle is vulnerable to attack, the patient was vulnerable to infection, his generous nature made him vulnerable to manipulation.

To avoid injury or attack or being taken advantage of, we developed armour. We placed the gentlest and most sensitive parts of ourselves under lock and key. We put up walls and barriers and fences to keep the aggressors away. The pity being, of course, that armour and locks and walls keep everyone away.

In her book *Daring Greatly*, Brené Brown defines vulnerability as 'uncertainty, risk and emotional exposure', all of which feel scary. But she also writes that 'vulnerability is the birthplace of love, belonging, joy, courage and creativity. It is the source of hope, empathy, accountability and authenticity.' Seems like a pretty sweet deal to me. Discomfort, risk and exposure for love, joy, creativity and hope.

Perhaps, however, this feels like too much and you find yourself already withdrawing from the idea of more connection. Maybe you've tried smiling at people you don't know, or spent time trying to radiate openness in a new place or tried going deep in a conversation with a friend, and maybe you haven't had the response you hoped for. Maybe your smile was ignored or sneered at, or your intent questioned. Maybe your deeper question or attempt at engagement fell on deaf ears. Maybe the person in the lift ignored you or you found yourself sidling up to a group of strangers at a networking event, trying to insert yourself smoothly into their conversation only to freeze up and slowly walk away backwards à la Bridget Jones (v. embarrassing).

It's okay. How are we ever meant to know the warm glow of true connection if we haven't felt the brutal sting of rebuke? We'd have nothing to compare it to.

And it is a sting. Even a rejection of the gentlest and smallest of outreaches can feel exceedingly harsh. Being seen and judged to be lacking in some capacity is the most human of hurts because it unearths those brutal words we say to ourselves and shines a light of truth on them. I'm not worthy. I don't belong here. I'm not good enough—I know it and now they know it too.

That sting often sees me react with defensiveness, out of shame or embarrassment from having 'put myself out there' only to be ignored or made to feel small and stupid. Then I move on to blaming the other person, sneering that it's actually their loss that they ignored my smile, and goodness me they must be so mean-spirited.

The truth is rarely as black and white, and nowhere near as interesting. Sure, it could be that my face did annoy them, or they hated me at first sight. More likely, though, is that they didn't see me (even if they looked my way) or were so caught up in what they were thinking about (which is probably not me) that I didn't even register with them.

Regardless, their reaction is okay. So is mine. It's all okay and it's all human. What these reactions speak to is our fear of vulnerability and the shame we experience when our vulnerability isn't met with kindness or even acknowledgement.

Instead of allowing the fear of vulnerability to harden our hearts and the ego to run roughshod over our attempts to connect, I'd encourage you to view the following experiments as gentle ways to dip your toe into vulnerability and her benefits. Ultimately it doesn't

the warm glow of true connection

matter who you connect with or how. You might choose to connect with your partner or child, a therapist or a friend, a beloved pet—or someone else's beloved pet for that matter, as looking into the eyes of an animal we like and trust can release oxytocin, thereby reducing stress and anxiety and improving our immune function—the only thing that matters is that you recognise that the vulnerability you may feel is deeply human, and that connection so often lies on the other side.

Eye contact

Eye contact is something humans both long for and fear. It opens us up to be seen, but at the same time it *opens us up to be seen* and oh god, what if they don't like what they see? What if I'm lacking? What if they laugh or smirk or ignore me? If you're looking for vulnerability, you can find it by the bucketload in human eye contact.

This vulnerability is precisely why eye contact plays a critical role in the development of our emotional connections and is one of the simplest ways to show someone that you acknowledge them, that you value them or that you're listening to them.

Now, I'm not talking about maintaining creepy levels of intense eye contact with total strangers. In fact, too much eye contact can be overwhelming for the person you're looking at, resulting in less connection, not more. Plus, it's important to remember that there are cultures in which maintaining strong eye contact can be seen as aggressive or rude.

What I'm talking about is a gentle prolonging of the daily eye contact you already make with people you know, or an effort to gradually increase your eye contact with strangers. This can have far-reaching benefits, including a release of the feel-good hormone oxytocin into our bloodstream. Even more importantly, it demonstrates to other humans that we recognise them as an individual and not just an obstacle on the footpath or another body on public transport. On some level I'd always known how important eye contact was, but in our Covid-affected world, as so many more of us wear masks on a regular basis, the eye-to-eye, human-to-human recognition is even more important. Where a smile might not be evident, friendly eye contact can bridge the gap.

Transactional interactions

Many of our day-to-day dealings with other people are transactional at best, so commonplace and insignificant that it's easy to miss them completely. The barista who makes your coffee, the colleague you half-smile at in the lift, the bus driver, the person at the supermarket checkout—you're both taking part in simple daily interactions but each of you is motivated by different reasons. One of you is working, the other needs caffeine, for instance. However, just because they're simple and insignificant in the grand scheme of things doesn't mean we can't use these interactions as an opportunity to connect more with the people around us, even if you're someone who makes it a habit to not engage in small talk. It's so easy to centre ourselves in the universe, believing that our problems are enormous while forgetting that others have problems that are just as pressing to them. Paying attention to these small, everyday interactions allows us to recognise other people as humans and to understand that *we* are a very tiny part of *their* day. We rationally understand this, of course, but actively acknowledging it teaches us humility and provides perspective and an ability to see other people's choices and reactions not as a response to us but as a response to things that may be happening in their life.

Think of a time when a stranger—a customer, a nurse, someone lining up in front of you at the movies—made you feel seen, when they asked a genuine question or looked you in the eye and smiled. Have you got a memory in mind? Can you recall where you were or how you felt? The fact that you remember such a small interaction shows how impactful they can be, don't you think?

My mum once told me a story about a customer, a young man, who regularly would come into the post office where she worked. He came in every week and paid $5 off his mobile phone bill. One day Mum mentioned that she thought it was great he was paying his bill regularly and reassured him that he'd pay it off soon. Each week they connected, ever so briefly, ever so transactionally, as human beings. On one particular day he paid his bill, she wished him a good day, and he left. A few hours later he walked back into the post office and walked up to Mum's counter. He told her that he'd been having a tough time lately and that her encouragement and kindness meant far more than she could ever know. With tears in his eyes, he thanked her and left.

It's a small story. One that probably plays out in similar ways millions of times a day all over the world. To me it's also proof that true connection, even of the briefest kind, has powerful, unseen ripples.

Smiling

Smiling at people is another simple act that can feel incredibly vulnerable. What if my smile is not reciprocated? What if the person I smile at innocently takes the wrong meaning? What if I have food in my teeth?

Okay, sure, these are possibilities, but what if you catch the eye of a stranger on the street, pass them a smile and have it returned to you at full brightness? What if you share a moment of genuine connection? What if you both walk away feeling seen? What if that moment of connection boosts your mood for the day and has a positive flow-on effect to your confidence, work or relationships? What if it has a similar positive flow-on effect for them? Who's to say where those ripples will extend?

Smiling can be one of the most effective ways of bringing down barriers between people. Busting out a grin, even when we may not strictly feel like it, also does amazing things to our brains by releasing neurotransmitters—including dopamine, serotonin and endorphins—that reduce stress and negative emotions such as frustration and anger, while also boosting positive emotions such as happiness. Smiling also reduces our blood pressure, which means we're better equipped to deal with stressful situations and, when paired with laughter, appears to boost our immune system by releasing signalling molecules in our brain that fight both stress and illness. Research by the University of Oxford has also found that laughter causes our bodies to release natural painkillers, which increases our tolerance to pain.

Additionally, and importantly as so many of us live with regular bouts of loneliness and isolation, smiling more can improve our existing relationships and help us to form new ones. People who smile often are perceived as more open, more likeable and more trustworthy, which means the likelihood of creating and maintaining better relationships is higher. Personally, I know that when I make a conscious effort to smile more, I'm much more likely to strike up a conversation or get a friendly smile in return (and I say this as a perfectly nice person with a significant case of Resting Bitch Face—if I can manage it, so can you).

This might feel a little insincere or inauthentic, but it's really not. Nor is any of this about faking it 'til you make it or repressing negative feelings. Our negative feelings are valid and if you have them, it's important to honour them and allow yourself to feel them, but if you're looking for another way of connecting with people and

Bring your attention and effort to being fully present, being supportive and being open to what the other person is saying.

experiencing some of the benefits of more human interaction, try smiling just once more than you otherwise would today. Walking down the street, in line at the petrol station, when you see your kids first thing in the morning and you're all sleepy and grumpy, when your partner gets home, when someone is looking for conflict—try a smile. And just notice what, if anything, happens.

Having said that, please, please don't use any of this as justification for demanding a smile from someone else. 'Give us a smile, love, it's not that bad' is not going to endear you to anyone, believe me.

Deep listening

As those hipsters of old, Simon and Garfunkel, told us back in 1964, there are a lot of people hearing without listening. It took me a while to work out the difference, but I think it's an important one to understand. For those of us who have the ability to hear, hearing is something we do a lot of. When we have a conversation with someone, we hear words and sounds and we process them. We understand the words we hear and interact accordingly.

Listening, however, is something we choose to do. It requires concentration and focus and a decision to pay attention to and carefully process the information we're receiving. Being a good listener is also something we need to practise, but the benefits make it a practice worth pursuing because deep listening can help us become more empathetic by allowing us to better understand the motives, needs and fears of the people we interact with. Over time this helps us develop a much fuller picture of who they are as human beings, which in turn improves our relationships by developing respect and trust. Deep listening is also believed to boost our confidence and self-esteem *because* of those improved relationships, and in a win for the time-poor among us, good listeners benefit from briefer conversations due to increased accuracy and improved understanding, meaning we spend less time repeating ourselves or re-hashing old information.

Better relationships? More trust and cooperation? Save time? More empathy? Imagine the collective impact of these changes in your life, in your family, in your community.

So how do you become a better listener? Next time you're having a conversation, try to focus closely on what the person you're speaking to is actually saying, rather than the narrative you're hearing in your head. You could try to resist the temptation to interrupt, judge or jump to conclusions. You can also bring your attention and effort to being fully present, being supportive and being open to what the other person is saying. Ultimately, deep listening is a choice and a practice, one where you can learn to come to conversations with the intention to listen rather than just hear.

Touch

Touch is powerful. And while it can, of course, be used in negative or manipulative ways, it is also a potent tool for bringing connection, healing, love and empathy to our relationships. We can use touch to soothe or comfort or show support. We hug and hold hands and smooth hair off hot foreheads. We wipe tears and squeeze shoulders and let our hips bump into another person's as we sit next to each other on the school bus. We can electrify and titillate and placate and show kindness with touch.

One of the barely acknowledged tragedies of Covid lockdown was the physical isolation many people experienced. People who lived by themselves, people with compromised immune systems, people who lived in care homes where empathetic or familial touch was scarce even before the pandemic, were thrown into a situation where they experienced hardly any or no touch at all. When I spend a moment considering it, I can feel this lack deep in my heart.

Can you imagine living for months devoid of hugs or a reassuring hand pat?

Touch deprivation, or skin hunger as it's sometimes known, is a very real condition that arises when we have little or no physical contact with others. It can result in an increase in aggressive behaviour, body-image issues, stress levels and loneliness, as well as high levels of tension, depression and anxiety.

When we're not living in a pandemic, the cure for many of us is a relatively simple one: to allow ourselves to experience more friendly or empathetic touch (from a person we feel safe with). Even the most everyday, incidental gestures—a pat on the back or a brief touch of the arm—are far more powerful than we might have imagined. Touch activates our brain's orbitofrontal cortex, which is linked to feelings of reward and compassion, and it can also trigger the release of oxytocin (our friendly love hormone popping up again), which is responsible for developing feelings of connection, love and bonding. Touch helps us to develop cooperation and, within the bounds of safe relationships, can also signal security and trust. If you've ever had someone you trust gently pat your back as you lay in bed as a child (or as an adult, for that matter), you know that empathetic touch can soothe beyond words. Interestingly, patients in palliative care experience that same response: research in 2012 by Dr William Collinge showed that patients are soothed by touch due to the related boost of oxytocin and the natural painkiller effect it has in the body. To connect with a gentle touch is to care.

I have very distinct memories of both my grandmother and grandfather getting comfort from holding our hands in their final days. It was an incredibly important experience for me to sit quietly with them one last time, their hand in mine, allowing us each to be comforted and soothed by the other. Seen and felt and loved. I also have distinct memories of times when a friend has given me the deep, meaningful kind of hug I needed, one that fills up some unseen part of me, one that leaves me in no doubt that I am supported. No words needed, touch conveys so much, so simply. A gentle pressure on the shoulder, a pat on the hand, a squeeze of the arm, a kiss on the top of a head; empathetic touch improves our quality of life, as well as, I suppose, our quality of death.

In times of isolation, however, it can be harder to find opportunity for these kinds of touch. In these instances, self-touch offers many of the same benefits as receiving touch from others, because any kind of gentle pressure on the skin releases many of the same chemicals as hugging or hand holding. So wrapping yourself tightly in a blanket or hugging a stuffed toy or pillow offer similar benefits, as does gentle yoga or cuddling with a pet.

It's my hope that, as the world moves towards whatever comes after Covid, it includes a much greater understanding of just how vital touch is to us—to our health, happiness and ability to thrive. I hope that we see a reset of aged and disability care, that we remember the value of a hug, that we invite our friends who live alone to stay with us more often.

Disconnect

I know that I said this book isn't written to demonise technology, but there's no hiding the reality that our screens are highly distracting and will relentlessly take our attention away from the physical world and the people in it, if we allow them to.

So, if we're talking about connection, it's important to talk about putting the tech down and looking up at people in the physical world—specifically at people you love. (Remember that Unplug tool?)

We've probably all been that person at the dinner table or party, checking our phone when we could have been talking or listening or people-watching. It's comfortable and easy to drift back to the digital world when we're bored or anxious or shy or feeling awkward.

A few years ago, I found myself in New York City's Central Park one spring day, around lunchtime. I'd spent a lot of time wandering around the city by myself that morning and was overwhelmed by the noise and busyness and people and concrete. What I needed was a green respite.

I found a bench in the sun and spent a few minutes looking up at the green buds on the oak trees that were just about to burst into the first leaves of the season. I looked at the daffodils and crocuses in full bloom. I watched the people moving past me, jogging or rollerblading, walking with friends, holding hands, laughing or talking. I watched the horse-drawn carriages pull people through the park as their guides pointed out the *Ghostbusters* building and Strawberry Fields while tourists filmed it all on their phones. Sometimes I wonder how many of those videos ever get looked at again. Maybe once or twice if they're posted to social media. Beyond that, are they cherished or are they a tick in a box on the Things I Have Done and Things I Have Seen list?

As I sat and watched, a woman rode her bike alongside one of these carriages. She turned her head towards the people in the back of the carriage, smiled widely at them even though their faces were glued to their screens and shouted, 'Get off your fucking phones and look up! You're missing life,' before speeding up and out of their day. Would I have said it? Probably not. Am I glad she did? Absolutely. (On a related note, I love New York.)

Reconnect

There is a particular joy when we reconnect with a friend from worlds past: it feels a little like a homecoming. Obviously, there are friendships that begin and end for valid reasons, but if you find yourself returning to thoughts of an old friend again and again, perhaps it's a sign that you should try to get in touch.

One of the benefits of connection tech is that it makes this kind of (potentially awkward) contact much, much easier, and the worst that can happen is an ignored email or Facebook message. No harm, no foul.

The other possibility is that they do get in touch, would like to reconnect, and this delivers you one of the most satisfying feelings that can arise in friendships—the sense that while decades may have passed, nothing has really changed. Having done this myself a few times over the last couple of years, feeling known and accepted in that way brought a wave of joy I rode for months.

So, if there is a face or a name that keeps coming back to you, perhaps ask yourself what might happen if you got in touch with them or, more importantly, why not embrace the not-knowing and ask yourself what you have to lose by trying?

Show up

Everyone has family, be it biological or chosen. If we're lucky, these are people with whom we feel truly seen and supported. We get so caught up in the keeping-up-appearances of our busy world that the important things get shuffled off to the side too often. Calling our parents, spending quality time with our kids or siblings, responding to messages from friends. Do we take for granted this unit, which has been in place for so long as to seem infallible? Do we expect that it will always be there? That there will always be tomorrow to make the call, to meet for a coffee, to go for a drive to their house and bring something for afternoon tea?

At the time of writing, my daughter is ten and my son is nine. Last night I lay down in bed with them one at a time until they fell asleep. It's not something I do very often, maybe once every couple of

Build connection with
your loved ones, creating
new memories that will
stretch and fill time.

months if that, but as I lay there last night, listening to their breaths slowly deepen and lengthen, I realised that I don't have too many more opportunities left to do this with them. At ten, our daughter might give me two more years before the inevitable and bittersweet distance that adolescence brings. Two years of lying with her at night once every couple of months equals maybe twelve more times spent being with her as she drifts off. Maybe double that for our son if I'm lucky. That's around thirty nights. That's *only* thirty nights.

As time continues to spool out, I could view this as devastating. Instead, I see it as an invitation to pay attention now. To soak it all in—the smells and sensations and knowing that I'm all in a moment. This thought applies to all of our closest relationships—we only have a finite number of phone calls, sleepovers, holidays or birthdays left to spend together. Consider this your invitation to show up for them.

This doesn't mean I plan to lie down with my kids every night and hum them to sleep. It does mean that when I'm all in, I'm *all* in. The same applies to any time we spend with people we love. We have a choice to phone it in or to go all-out. Soak it up. Pay attention to their faces, their eyes, the way they laugh.

Turning up, making eye contact, asking questions, learning to listen deeply, giving a hug—all of these actions can help you build connection with your loved ones, creating new memories that will stretch and fill time. The ones that will sustain us on the days when the hours slip by so fast that it makes our head spin.

What next?

All the ideas and experiments in this chapter are designed to help you connect with other people, whether by simply acknowledging them and the fact that they have stories and worries and joys just like you, by deepening the relationships you already have, or by creating and building new ones over time. Some will help you build intimacy; others will help you feel part of something much larger and more significant. My only hope is that there is one suggestion on these pages that sticks with you. One that sparks some light of recognition in you, that feels powerful. When you find that one thing, play with it. Explore it and observe yourself as you do. How do you feel when thinking about it? When you do it? After you've finished? Take note of those feelings and use them as motivation to try again or try something else.

The song tells us we're all in this together, and while I'm not convinced that everyone believes that, I am convinced that the vast majority of us are doing the best we can with what we've got. And for those of us who aren't, well, I believe that connecting with other human beings, really seeing each other, will help us to do better.

IF YOU HAVE HALF A MINUTE

- Once a day, gently prolong your gaze with a loved one, extending it slightly beyond the length you would normally hold their gaze for.
- When someone is talking to you, put down your phone, close your laptop, turn off the TV and look at them.
- Look up and try to make eye contact with the people you walk past.
- In a transactional interaction, be interested in the other person and ask how their morning has been or if they had a good weekend, then listen to their reply.
- Hold hands with someone.
- Look into the eyes of a beloved pet (or someone else's).
- Give someone a long, deep, heartfelt hug just because.
- Link arms with a friend or put your arm around the shoulder of your partner.

IF YOU HAVE HALF AN HOUR

- Give or receive a massage, or give yourself a massage on your scalp, hands, feet or shoulders.
- Practise yoga.
- Try eye gazing—where you sit quietly across from another person and spend time simply gazing into their eyes.

- Schedule a video call with someone who lives far from you.
- Play Twenty Questions with a friend and find out things you never knew about them.
- Record your parents talking about their earliest memories, their thoughts about the world today, the happiest day of their lives.
- Make a time for a weekly phone call with your mum and stick with it.
- Write a letter to someone you love and put it in the mail.

IF YOU HAVE HALF A DAY OR MORE

- Take a class with your friends—learning how to do something new together helps develop intimacy.
- Go on a long walk with your family and leave your phones at home (yes, all of you).
- Challenge your family or housemates to a screen-free day and spend it making things, playing games, going for walks and reading out loud.
- Build something: a piece of furniture, a fort, a bike track.
- Do a jigsaw puzzle or play a boardgame with loved ones.

CHAPTER 2

kindness

Do you see?

How a hand gently held

a wall deftly felled

a wave freely offered

a burden shared, not suffered

an hour gladly spent

an ear kindly lent

a meal happily prepared

a bounty joyfully shared

a smile shyly slanted

is a seed lovingly planted.

Do you see?

How it germinates

in the warm, dark space

just below your heart.

Do you see?

How it blossoms and fruits,

scattering seeds,

leaving a trail of blooms

with every footstep.

Do you see?

I've always loved words.

The way a seemingly arbitrary sequence of letters can add up to create meaning. The way a series of words combine to paint pictures in my mind, and how they can travel vast distances in space and time to connect people and ideas and stories.

I have a soft spot for whimsical words (balderdash, curmudgeonly, shenanigans) and onomatopoeia (plop and fizz and splash and blurt). There are phonesthemic words (churlish, sludge and twinkle), which embody their meaning through their sound alone, otherwise described by Terry Pratchett in his novel *The Wee Free Men* as 'a word that sounds like the noise a thing would make if that thing made a noise even though, actually, it doesn't, but would if it did'. Glitter. Snicker. Slobber. Gleam.

I love learning about words that have no English equivalent. Words like *komorebi*, a Japanese noun for sunlight filtering through trees, or *mångata*, a Swedish word for the glimmering, road-like reflection the moon creates on smooth water. There is the Urdu noun *goya*, which means the suspension of disbelief that occurs while listening to good storytelling, or *hiraeth*, the Welsh word that covers a homesickness for a home you can't return to, or that never was.

Some words sound harsh (buzz, cough, grind), some cause a visceral reaction (moist, ointment, phlegm), while others feel soft and round and comforting (cuddle, rainbow, snuggle).

Then there are words that don't always quite seem to fit their meaning, words like *kind*.

On one hand, it fits perfectly because kind sounds nice, affable and avuncular. Kind speaks of Mr Rogers, as though someone with a lived-in face and twinkling eyes is smiling at you, reading to you, handing you something warm to drink. Kind is small, gentle and round somehow.

On the other hand, kindness can be a world-changing idea, one that is powerful and transformative, and in that capacity, the word itself has always felt a little . . . flaccid. Did I really think such a soft and gentle four-letter word was capable of changing a world that seems to be getting colder, meaner and more divided? A world where politicians spend more time eviscerating each other than governing, where divisions are growing deeper and more hate-filled, where the comments sections of websites and social-media posts are often a hotbed of faceless cruelty—petty or otherwise.

To be honest, the instruction to 'try kindness' in the face of all that callousness has often felt like throwing flowers at an attacking crocodile or spitting on a bushfire.

This is not to say that I don't believe in kindness. On the contrary, I've always espoused kindness as important. I've brought my kids up to be kind. I've experimented with doing one random act of kindness every day and I've been surprised by the impact it had on me. But deep down, in my heart, did I really believe that kindness could change the world?

Not really. It might change a mood. Change a day. Change a life even. But the world? I couldn't see it. Kind never seemed powerful enough.

Covid made me reconsider. As we saw random and beautiful acts of kindness play out around the world during lockdown, I could see how even simply observing those acts had a unifying effect on us, how they rippled out and made waves and, just as importantly, how they made us realise that while there is pain and hatred in the world, there is also extraordinary generosity, altruism and love.

I started reading about kindness, what it is, how it affects us, how it can transform, and what I discovered is that while kindness may have a soft, comforting skin, forgiving and soothing to touch, at its core is pure steel, strong enough to break down barriers, bring down walls, and lift up the heaviest and most heartbroken of us. (What I think I've actually discovered is that kindness is like Baymax, the inflatable helper robot from the Disney film *Big Hero 6*: a huge, soft, marshmallow on the outside, so comforting to look at, so reassuring to sink into, but at its centre is a carbon-fibre skeleton so tough it can withstand superhuman forces.)

I had made the mistake of thinking that something so universally available as to appear entirely unspecial couldn't possibly be that powerful, when that's precisely where its power comes from. We all have kindness at our disposal at any moment of any day.

I used to believe that we needed hard edges to get through life. That brute force and armour were necessary to succeed, or even to come out okay. That we needed to be a little less Baymax, a little more Terminator. Now I think the reason we so readily ignore the power of kindness is because it makes us uncomfortable. There is vulnerability in kindness, a softness that feels incredibly foreign because so many of us are deficient in *self*-kindness. We don't really know how to love ourselves, and as Brené Brown writes in her book *The Gifts of Imperfection*, 'We can only love others as much as we love ourselves.'

This idea kicked me square in the stomach the first time I read it. Not only because it seemed to tell me that my capacity to love the people I cared most about in the world was limited, but also because it unearthed a dreadful truth. I had no love for me, and I knew it. No care. No acceptance. Certainly no kindness. The notion of offering unconditional love and kindness to myself was so alien it felt jarring. I still get a lump in my throat thinking about it. How often have I truly shown myself kindness? Not in a 'Hey girl, let's have a face mask and a cup of tea' way, but in the way I might kneel down in front of a scared child and fold them gently into my arms, smoothing the hair off their clammy forehead, telling them quietly that I'm here and it's all going to be okay. When do any of us ever treat ourselves with that level of kindness and acceptance? What might change if we did?

So much of what we do and think and say, so much of the busyness that drives us, that keeps us from slowing down and connecting with others, from practising kindness, stems from a sense that we are not enough. Not good enough. Funny enough. Interesting enough. Successful or wealthy or attractive enough. So, we try to buy our enoughness, we dress ourselves in enoughness, we splash our enoughness all over social media. We tell our friends how enough we are when we describe how hectic life has been. We dive into the to-dos and to-buys of self-care, self-help, self-improvement in the hope that we will 'fix' ourselves and then, only then, will we be enough. Maybe. For a little while.

Here's the thing. You're not broken. You don't need fixing. Any 'thing', any purchase, any -ism, any book or article or influencer that makes you think you are, is not being kind. What we all need is to learn how to feel accepted and supported from within because if we don't feel like our own safe place then it's going to be really tough to offer that to anyone else. In other words, if we don't have a reserve of self-kindness and self-acceptance, how can we ever imagine a world where we regularly extend those things to others—let alone one where that kindness and acceptance changes the fabric of society.

This begs the question: how can we learn to be kind to ourselves when our default is the opposite? I don't know about you, but I've always been scared to show myself kindness. As though letting my foot off my throat for a moment will allow me to get away with being a bit shit or lazy or no good. Or that I will collapse completely under the realisation that I'm operating with no love, and the

Here's the thing.
You're not broken.
You don't need fixing.

longest-lasting relationship of my life is built on a foundation
of indifference at best, hatred and loathing at worst.

Now, I'm no psychologist, nor a psychiatrist. I have spent my
fair share of time with a number of them, but that's where my
experience ends, so take what follows with a grain of salt and a
hearty dose of Please Speak to Someone if You're Struggling. (It's
okay to do that. You're not weak and there's nothing wrong with you.
We all need help getting back up sometimes, and at some stage will
all need a reminder that we are worthy of love and kindness. Yes,
that includes you. Yes, you. The one reading this right now thinking
it doesn't. It does.) What I've noticed about kindness is that we have
a natural tendency to tenderness, until we look in the mirror. Our
ability to forgive and accept and support the people we love runs out
when it comes to offering the same gift to ourselves, which means
that at some point we start drawing from an empty well and instead
of kindness, we begin pulling up exhaustion, or resentment, or
experiencing burnout instead.

Picture this

Are you ready to do a little exercise in imagining? If you are, I'd
like you to imagine two things.

First, bring to mind a problem, mistake or failure you've been
carrying around with you. Something that makes you feel like you're
not good enough. It doesn't matter if this thing is big or small, new
or old, you'll know the kind I'm talking about because it will give
you that uncomfortable, hot, squirmy feeling in your stomach and
will bring you a sense of regret or shame or embarrassment. Once
you have this problem in mind, I want you to imagine picking it up
and putting it in a box. The regret, the failure, the stress or pain, the
stick you're beating yourself with, whatever it is, put it in a box and
then put a lid on the box.

Now imagine standing face to face with someone you love. A friend, a partner, a mentor, a parent or a sibling. Just choose one. One you love. One you support and accept and for whom you want nothing but happiness and health and contentment.

Once you have your person in mind, imagine passing the box to them and, as you do so, the problem in it becomes theirs. They now have full ownership of the box and everything that comes with it. The guilt, the shame, the regret, it's now something your loved one has to carry with them. As you look at them for a moment maybe you can see their face is now pinched with anxiety, or perhaps they're crying or struggling with the weight of the box, their shoulders slumped and their eyes downcast.

You can see the struggle, you can empathise with them, you want to comfort them and offer them what they need, so you take a step back and ask yourself, 'What would I say to this person right now, to make them feel loved, supported and accepted?' Think about which words they'd need to hear from you in order to lighten that load, and consider what you have to offer in compassion, acceptance and love.

Okay. If you've got that scene in mind, I want you to hold it for a moment. Let yourself feel it.

While you do that, let's take a peek at the scene inside my head. (It's a bit of a mess in here, sorry. Mind the stacks of notebooks and empty coffee mugs.)

Here you can see I'm picturing a dear friend. She's going through a tough time, feeling overwhelmed by life right now, buckling under the weight of difficult circumstances, most of which are completely beyond her control. She's struggling with unrealistic expectations and comparisons, mostly self-imposed, and she's using them as bullet points in her very long list of Reasons Why She's A Failure and Sucks at Everything. My friend can't find any kindness for herself, nor any acceptance. Only a mountain of judgement and criticism.

What do I say to this friend? How can I show her that she's not alone, that she is accepted, supported and, no matter what, she is loved? Perhaps I could tell her that she's doing better than she thinks and the reason she can't see that is because her inner critic has taken over. I could tell her that literally no one has their shit together like Instagram would have her believe. That some days her best won't be all that good, but even that's okay. Perhaps I would hold her close. I would let her cry. I would walk with her along a quiet riverside path, my arm in hers, as I listen. I would not offer solutions. I would not tell her that everything will be fine. I would encourage her to simply look for the next step. I would tell her that if she can't see it, then she only needs to look for a smaller step because there will always be one.

I would tell her that right now, even though she doesn't feel it, she is enough.

This, I can do. Offering this level of support and love to a friend feels natural, necessary. What doesn't feel so easy is the next step I'm going to take. I look a little closer at the face of this friend and step towards her, and as I do this, I realise that I'm looking in a mirror. It's my own face I'm staring at, and now I'm forced to admit that the heavy weight she is carrying is mine, and the words of acceptance and love I just offered her are, in reality, being directed at me. From me.

It's amazing how quickly the feeling changes. From unconditional love and acceptance to something much sharper and meaner. Suddenly it feels stupid and wrong to offer myself kindness in this way. We're shown over and over again—in advertising, social media, the competitive and combative and shallow TV shows we watch, the magazines we read—why we're not good enough, and it's little wonder we've internalised that disdain. If we are what we eat and we've been fed a steady diet of stories about why we don't deserve kindness (until we're wealthy or skinny or successful or famous enough), then it makes sense that I'm suddenly very confused when I realise that the face in the mirror is my own.

Still, part of me knows that the support and compassion I directed at the woman in the mirror can't be taken back, not when it was offered so freely just a moment ago. That would mean that either I was lying to my friend, and she isn't worthy of my support, or I'm lying to myself in saying that I'm not.

Now, I want you to give it a try. Return to the scene in your mind. Look at that loved one across from you, the one holding your problem as their own. The one chastising themselves and beating themselves up. Tell them what they need to hear. Tell them how much you love them, tell them that no matter how much they've messed up, you accept them and are with them. Tell them until they believe you. Then look a little closer at them, closer and closer still, until you realise that it's you you're talking to. It's you holding this problem and it's you you're now offering compassion to. Then you need to decide—were you lying to your friend or lying to yourself? Both can't be true at the same time. They can't be worthy while you aren't. Either neither of you deserve kindness, or you both do.

It's kind of heavy-handed. But self-compassion is worth exploring because so much of our ability to spread kindness in the world hinges on our capacity to give ourselves some of the same. That's easier said than done, though, isn't it? If you're thinking this exercise feels a little intense, then what else can we do to gradually foster our self-kindness practice? (It is a practice; those muscles of compassion won't get any stronger until we start using them regularly.)

You can learn to be kind to yourself by carving out a little bit of time every day to do something you like. It might be five minutes to draw or garden or do your make-up in a way that makes you feel good. The typical self-help offerings of journalling or creating

the face in the mirror is my own

positive affirmations and repeating them to yourself every day are also ways to build that self-kindness muscle. (I spent three months telling myself, out loud, every morning, 'I am allowed to take up space. I will take up space. I gladly take up space' until I believed it.)

Taking a moment to celebrate an achievement is also an act of self-kindness. If you ran all the way to the top of the hill near your house, celebrate with a Rocky-style fist pump. If you nailed the presentation at work, give yourself a 'Hell yes you did' in the mirror afterwards. Conjure up an inner advocate (mine is Jonathan Van Ness from *Queer Eye*), who is full of encouragement and kindness and who gives you permission to feel good about the things you do, no matter how small or seemingly insignificant.

You could also take a moment every night to think about something you did that day that made you proud. It might be as small (or large) as getting out of bed when all you wanted to do was stay under the covers, or dealing with a discipline issue without losing your cool. Maybe you drank eight glasses of water or went for a walk at lunch. Perhaps you called a mate or picked up a few pieces of rubbish while your kids were at soccer training. Don't undervalue yourself. The things you do matter and by extending that small nod of kindness towards yourself day after day, you might find that you begin to look for more opportunities for kindness as time goes on, and those waves will just keep rolling out from you when you do.

Another really powerful way we can develop self-kindness is by doing things for others. While that might sound like it's going to benefit the person receiving your kindness rather than you as the giver, there's something very magical you should know about kindness. It's one of the few things in the world that doubles, or sometimes even triples, when you give it away.

The receiver of kindness benefits, as does the person giving the kindness, but so too does someone who simply observes an act of kindness. So, if you offer your seat to someone on the bus, they benefit, as do you. In addition, the body and brain of any other passenger on that bus who sees your interaction will respond almost as though they've been the one to receive the kindness themselves. What's more, giving, receiving or observing kindness makes us far more likely to turn around and do more kind things ourselves, as shown in a 2016 Stanford University study published in *Scientific American*. All of which adds up to one thing: kindness breeds kindness.

If you consider this in real terms, you can see how one small act of random kindness, given, received and observed, can move through a community like ripples from a pebble tossed into a pond, reaching out in greater and greater circles.

Whether that pebble is big or small, impressively splashy or quiet, hardly matters because the ripples are real. So too are the physical and emotional benefits that make kindness so powerful, which remain the same no matter how small the act.

Even one small random act of kindness a day has been shown to:

- **boost levels of oxytocin, which in turn reduces our blood pressure and improves our overall heart health**
- increase our levels of self-esteem and feelings of optimism
- **help you feel stronger and more energetic**
- give you a greater sense of calm and increased feelings of self-worth
- **light up the reward and pleasure centre of your brain, as though you are actually the person receiving the kindness—a phenomenon called the 'helper's high'**
- stimulate the production of serotonin, which helps us to heal more quickly while also increasing feelings of calm

- produce endorphins—your brain's own natural painkiller—resulting in less physical pain
- reduce the levels of cortisol (your stress hormone), which not only offers the benefit of fewer symptoms of stress but also helps us to age more slowly
- significantly increase positive moods and offer a similarly significant reduction in anxiety levels, even in those of us who are highly anxious
- significantly reduce inflammation levels in the body, particularly in people over 55.

What would happen if we made a habit of kindness? If we made it a daily practice, like gratitude or stretching or drinking water? How would that pond, still rippling from the impact of one pebble, be transformed by more of them? Imagine how a handful cast into the water would create many more tiny waves that overlap and bump against each other, making even more ripples, changing the surface of the pond, affecting every inch of it.

Let's take the Covid crisis for example. In the early days there was a lot of footage emerging of people hoarding and fighting over toilet paper and bags of rice. Fear and greed seemed to be contagious. Almost simultaneously, I began to see more acts of selfless generosity and kindness unfolding around me. In our small town, buckets of flowers and strawberry plants appeared at the end of driveways, one of them accompanied by a sign, 'Take one if you need a lift ☺', and on the local Facebook page, residents organised a roster for checking in on elderly neighbours. There was a drive-by birthday parade for a little boy whose party was cancelled, and we saw rainbows and teddy bears appear in windows all over town, a reminder that within each house were people just like us, living through the same strange times, staying home out of a desire to

One random act
of kindness can start
a chain reaction
that spreads across
classrooms,
workplaces, towns
and communities.

care for and protect each other. When public housing towers in Melbourne were locked down, I saw stories of police officers walking residents' dogs and other residents banding together to translate public health information into ten languages overnight, to ensure that their neighbours were kept updated. We saw cities all over the world stop every night to applaud their healthcare workers and British centenarian Captain Tom Moore trying to raise £1000 for the NHS by walking laps of his backyard. We saw how his kindness was met with the kindness of others as he went on to raise more than £33 million. One random act of kindness can start a chain reaction that spreads across classrooms, workplaces, towns and communities. Is it so outlandish to imagine that this very same chain reaction could spread to cover our cities, our states, our countries, the entire world even?

Why not experiment with kindness and see how you feel? Regardless of how much time, energy, money or access you do or don't have, there is always a kindness you can offer. Keep reading for some ideas to get you started.

IF YOU HAVE HALF A MINUTE

▼

- Write a love note to your partner or kids and pop it in their work bag or lunchbox.

- Leave a handwritten note for a stranger to find saying something that you've needed to hear in the past. 'You're doing better than you think you are' or 'You matter'.

- Leave a positive review for a bar, restaurant, store or service you appreciate.

- Compliment a stranger on their style or their smile.

- If you see someone trying really hard to get through their workout at the gym, give them some encouragement—a high five or a thumbs up.

- In traffic, if someone lets you in ahead of them, give them a courtesy wave, or let another car go in front of you.

- Look out for tiny ways to help a stranger—hold the door, offer to help a parent carry their pram up the stairs, assist someone with their bags.

- Tidy the office kitchen, or at least leave it a little nicer than you found it.

- Let a parent know that they're doing a good job.

- Offer to take a photo for a stranger who's trying to take a selfie.

- Ask the name of someone you frequently interact with (security guard at work, barista, bus driver etc.) and use it whenever you see them.

- Pick up rubbish on the street or at the beach.

- If you see a photo, song, meme, movie or joke that reminds you of a friend, send it to them, tell them that it made you think of them and take the opportunity to ask how they are.
- Make a cup of tea for someone.
- Just listen.

IF YOU HAVE HALF AN HOUR

- Plant a tree.
- Cut herbs or flowers from your garden and make a bouquet for a friend.
- If you're heading to the shops, ask your family or housemates if they need anything while you're out.
- Cook something for a friend or neighbour and drop it on their doorstep: a cake, some muffins, a loaf of bread, a pot of soup.
- Donate blood.
- If you see your neighbour working outside, make them a coffee or a cold drink and go sit with them in the sun.
- Shovel or sweep your neighbour's driveway.
- Make morning tea for your colleagues.
- Call your parents or grandparents just to check in.

IF YOU HAVE HALF A DAY OR MORE

▼

- Volunteer at your local soup kitchen, hospital, men's or women's shed, re-use and repair centre.

- Collect and recycle cans and bottles, and donate the money you make to a charity you want to support.

- Babysit a friend's child so they can take a walk, go to the gym or see a movie.

- Offer to repair something for a friend.

- Create a 'Little Free Library' and place it on your front fence, encouraging people to take a book and leave a book.

- Start a fundraiser for a cause you're passionate about.

- Challenge yourself to a 'judgement-free day', where you try to put compassionate, empathetic or kind thoughts out into the world.

- Go watch a friend's soccer match and cheer them on from the sidelines.

- Make a bird bath or a bird-feeding station and put it near the footpath so others can enjoy the birds who use it.

- Create and send a care package to a loved one who lives far away and include a note saying how much you miss them.

- Pack up your unwanted books and donate them to a library, asylum seeker centre or homeless shelter.

IF YOU CAN SHARE SOME MONEY

- Leave a copy of your favourite book on a park bench or on the train, with a note inside saying you hope it's as impactful for them as it was for you, and suggest they pass it forward when they finish.
- Pay for the coffee of the person in line behind you at the cafe.
- Donate to a local charity.
- Pay for feed at your local wildlife rescue service.
- Sponsor a newly arrived refugee or a child in a developing country.
- Calculate your annual carbon footprint and buy enough tree-planting credits to offset it. Then make one change that will result in a lower footprint next year.

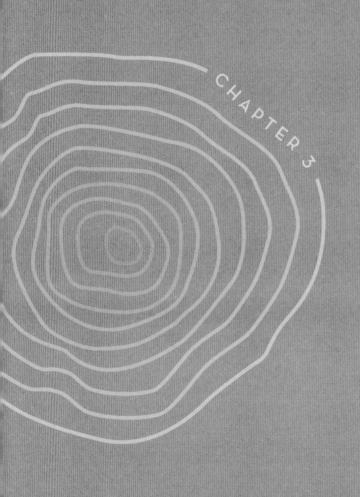

CHAPTER 3

awe

Born of fire

We begin, dark, alone

Floating in the void

until, by some invisible hand

parts drawn together, spinning

faster and faster

A spark ignites at the very centre—

we're forged, parts anew.

With life, small and quiet

Relentlessly inching closer

To grass, to blooms

To trees and rocks and rivers

To our tentative steps

Our halting breath

To love. To beauty.

To all things and all people,

To you. To me.

Made of stars.

Born of fire.

When I say 'awe' what do you picture?

Perhaps, like me, your mind's eye immediately conjures typically awe-inspiring images of things such as vast snow-capped mountains or dolphins frolicking near the shore of a pristine beach or the view from the edge of the Grand Canyon. You know, Big Nature.

There's no doubt that Big Nature *is* awe-inspiring. I count myself as very lucky to have seen some in my life and have felt the waves of awe sweep through me as a result. I've seen the Canadian Rockies rise from misty valleys; I've been in the surf when a pod of dolphins emerged to play in the waves nearby; I've stood motionless on the edge of the South Rim of the Grand Canyon one freezing January morning, fresh snow on the ground and ice on my eyelashes, watching the changing colours of the landscape as the sun rose.

But awe is much more complex than that and is a very tricky thing to define. According to the psychologists and scientists who study it at the University of California, Berkeley's Greater Good Science Centre, awe can be defined as 'the feeling we get in the presence of something vast that challenges our understanding of the world'. It's often described using words such as amazement, surprise or transcendence, or even more simply by Professor Dacher Keltner, leading researcher at UC Berkeley, as something that 'passes the goosebumps test'.

What those self-transcending, goosebump-providing experiences look like can vary wildly, and researchers believe that an awe-inspiring experience doesn't need to be big (or nature-based) in order to be powerful. It can be more intimate, more human, more commonplace and still fill you with awe. To that end I've also found awe in the sun spiking dusty, golden rays through a canopy of pine trees. I've felt it noticing the finest hairs on my son's cheeks. I've been awed by my daughter reading out loud to me and the first cherry I ever ate off the tree in our front yard, warm and soft from the sun, tasting of summer and victory because I'd gotten to it before the birds.

Awe can be found in great and majestic places, both natural and man-made, and it can be found in the smallest of everyday details. Palaces and sandcastles. Packed theatres and quiet compassion. Regardless of where you find it, the consensus is that awe can be an incredibly powerful force in our lives and, over the past twenty years, as the relatively new study of awe has grown steadily, scientists, researchers and psychologists have uncovered some impressive benefits to experiencing it, which include:

- improved moods
- higher levels of general life satisfaction
- reduced stress levels
- reduced inflammation
- improved critical-thinking abilities
- reduction in materialism
- a shift in self-perception, relative to humanity and the natural world
- increased sense of humility
- expansion in perception of time, making people feel like they have more of it to enjoy
- less impatience
- higher likelihood of giving time, energy or attention to others
- higher likelihood of wanting to cooperate with others
- more generosity.

If you took that list of benefits and inverted each item to its opposite, you'd be describing many of the deficiencies of modern life. We live in a highly individualistic society, with widespread overconsumption, record levels of stress-related health problems (both physical and mental), high levels of discontentment, impatience and a sense that no matter what we do, we never have enough hours in the day. In a culture where our worth is so often measured by the stuff we own, our physical appearance, our job title or income, the number of social-media followers we have or books we've sold, the sense of connection to something greater than ourselves that awe researchers describe feels thrillingly counter-cultural. So how can awe offer us an antidote to some of the stressors of modern life? How can it help us create slow, powerful ripples of change in our own lives, our families, our communities?

Think for a moment what the flow-on effects of each of the above benefits might mean to you, your relationships, your work, the world you live in. Think of how each of them could impact your ability and desire to care more. If experiencing awe delivers us an increase in generosity, for example, how might that impact my relationship with my husband? Maybe it means that I give a more genuine and specific offer of help one night when he's stressed, or maybe I listen more actively when he shares what's troubling him. Perhaps, in time, that means we see a gradual deepening of intimacy or a feeling of greater security in our relationship. That might then manifest in our tendency to care for each other in a new way or grow more trust or kindness or support. That in turn could flow out into our relationship with our kids, our extended family, and the work we do.

Or we can look at the sense of self-transcendence psychologists talk about when we experience awe. How might that blurring of the edges between myself and something greater impact me? Could it be that on the day I have an awe-inspiring experience, I view the strangers I cross paths with afterwards more as brothers and sisters in humanity rather than blips on my daily radar? And what might that change bring to me? Empathy or compassion in place of judgement or self-centring overreaction? A choice to see someone driving aggressively not as a personal affront (they're probably not trying to kill me) but as a response to something going on in their lives? And my choice to not respond with aggression or anger, as I may otherwise have done, could mean I arrive at my destination feeling calmer and more open to others, so I smile and make eye contact with the person who helps me at the library, which might send them on their own path of connection and kindness for the day.

Or, to think more broadly, consider this: Australia is a country of astounding natural beauty. From the red heart of Uluru to the ultramarine waters of Booderee National Park, the ancient forests of the Tarkine in Tasmania to some of the most diverse and unique wildlife in the world, there is no shortage of awe-inducing wonder in our country. Australia has also historically been one of the most generous countries in the world, ranking third in the Charities Aid Foundation report of charitable giving in 2015–16. Giving on average $12 billion a year, Australians were only out-generoused by Myanmar and the United States.

Given one of the by-products of experiencing more awe is a boost in generosity, I've often wondered if we, as a nation, are generous *because* we have so many opportunities for awe and, if so, why have we seen a reduction in generosity in recent years?

Our generous giving dropped by 10 per cent between 2016 and 2017 and, while there are a number of theories as to why that is, I can't help but wonder if we've lost some of our capacity for awe, robbing us of the sense of community, altruism, connection and cooperation that encourage us to give more generously. Maybe it's because we spend so much time on our tech that we forget to look up, maybe it's because we're more disconnected from our communities than ever, maybe it's because Australians spend far more time on screens than we used to. Is it possible that these shifts have taken the wind out of our generosity sails, leaving us more removed and less caring than before?

Wouldn't it then follow that a prescription of more awe in our daily lives may begin to reverse some of these changes?

I started writing the first draft of this book against the backdrop of the devastating Black Summer bushfires, the worst bushfire season on record. Thirty-four people died, thousands of homes were destroyed, more than a billion animals were killed and over 12 million hectares of Australian bush and rainforest was burnt. In a word, it was catastrophic. But even as the fires raged on, Australians mobilised to help in whatever way they could. Donations of food, clothes and bedding rolled into centres around the country, hundreds of millions of dollars were raised for volunteer firefighters who battled the fires for months on end, millions more were raised for the families and businesses that were directly affected. Comedian Celeste Barber rallied her fan base on Facebook and Instagram to raise more than $50 million—much of it from people who don't even live in Australia. It was astounding and affirming and unifying to see such an outpouring of generosity in the face of such awe-inspiring devastation, and equally as affirming to see the global community come together in such incredible ways.

Perhaps the use of the word awe struck you as a little off in that last sentence. So much of what we think of when we discuss awe is positive or beautiful, and pairing awe with destruction and devastation can feel a little jarring. According to Professor Dacher Keltner, there are actually five different 'flavours' of awe: beauty, achievement, virtue, the supernatural and, somewhat incongruently, threat. Awe can promote both positive and negative feelings but it's

interesting to note that even when the awe we feel is due to fear
or threat, the benefits we experience remain the same.

How can we harness the community/nation/world-changing
benefits of awe, without putting ourselves in the way of danger or
journeying to the most far-flung corners of the world, in search of
wondrous new experiences? What awe-inspiring things can you and
I do in our everyday lives that might help us become more generous
and community-minded? What can help us become humbler, more
patient, less stressed and less materialistic?

Virtues, abilities and accomplishments of others

We're surrounded by people who provide us with endless
opportunities for awe, if we choose to see it. Among the five different
kinds of awe Keltner says we experience, one is awe of virtue. We
experience this when we learn about or examine the life of someone
who displays virtue and strength of character. This might include
internal strength and discipline, strength in the face of adversity
or strength in advocating for themselves or others. Our world is
full of people who display awe-inspiring strengths.

Consider Kurt Fearnley, an Australian Paralympic champion
who was born with a congenital disorder called sacral agenesis,
which prevented foetal development of parts of his lower spine
and sacrum. As a result, Fearnley doesn't have the use of his legs.
In spite of this, in 2009, using only his arms and upper body, he
dragged himself the full length of the Kokoda Track in Papua New
Guinea—96 kilometres of incredibly steep, rough terrain, mud
and forests—to raise funds for men's mental health services.

Think of the frontline healthcare workers around the globe who
have worked relentlessly throughout the Covid pandemic, at great
risk not only to themselves, but also potentially to their family and
friends. Knowing the risks, these people still continued to show up

day after day, to work in incredibly difficult, oftentimes devastating circumstances in order to protect us. In some cases, even after they'd lost members of their own family to the pandemic.

Reflect on the research and experimentation, the discoveries and expertise that went into the development of the polio vaccine, the perseverance and diplomacy that went into the fall of the Berlin Wall, the work required to build Stonehenge, the mind-bending ingenuity of the people who created the pyramids in Egypt.

As a side note, I've sometimes found myself feeling bad about my own trivial-seeming efforts and achievements when I hear about the accomplishments of others (which probably says more about me than anything else), but if you find yourself feeling the same way, let me offer you some encouragement. We're looking for awe rather than comparison, and it can be found in very ordinary achievements too. There's no doubt humans can do great things. We can save hundreds of lives, go to the moon and invent incredible solutions for enormous problems. But we can also accomplish small, seemingly simple things that are, in fact, deceptively complex.

Next time you make yourself a sandwich, I want you to think about all the elements of that sandwich. The bread, the avocado, the cucumber and lettuce and tomato and carrot and salt and pepper. Where did the wheat in the bread come from? Who planted it? Who harvested it? How was it milled from wheat to flour? Who then took that flour and turned it into bread?

What about the avocado? Where did it come from? How many years has that farmer been growing avocados? How big is the tree it was picked from and who picked it?

What's the name of the person who grew the tomato, the carrot, the cucumber? Where were they grown? What needed to happen to get them from the vine or soil to the supermarket on the very day you bought them?

Just pause to consider all the people, processes and equipment that had to come together at the exact right time in order for you to be able to make your sandwich. Doesn't it make that first bite not only delicious but also kind of extraordinary?

Wonder

Awe has a sister and her name is wonder: she's the feeling of amazement and admiration you may encounter when experiencing something beautiful, remarkable or unfamiliar. She's a glorious, joy-filled thing, similar to awe in her capacity to shift our perspective, yet different in the way she makes us feel. While wonder often lives alongside curiosity and joy, awe can also bring us fear and respect. They're perfectly suited playmates, rounding out our experience of the world. We often look for them only in the grandest of grand sites but wonder and awe can be found everywhere—including the small, ignored places and the experiences we take for granted. So, keeping that in mind, and before we go off searching for these sisters at the Seven Wonders of the World, I want to start our awe experiment in the most familiar, most ignored and most taken-for-granted places— our own miraculous bodies.

If we're able to find moments and experiences of awe in our beautiful skin suits and all that happens inside them, we will never be without a reason for wonder. Even on the grimmest of days, the longest, loneliest of nights, you will have wonder and beauty and awe inside you—literally.

Your body

Your body is, without meaning to sound clichéd, an absolute miracle.

Did you know the average human body is made of approximately 37 trillion cells? To put that number into perspective, if you could

Awe can be found in
great and majestic
places, both natural and
man-made, and it can
be found in the smallest
of everyday details.

count ten of those cells every second it would take you *tens of thousands* of years to finish counting them.

Then consider that the vast majority of those 37 trillion cells cooperate with each other for decades, collectively creating a single, conscious, intelligent organism. This single, conscious, intelligent organism is capable of love and compassion and laughter and optimism and art. Organisms just like us have travelled to space, invented solar panels, painted masterpieces, written life-altering books and led movements that changed the world.

What's more, every human—no matter our heritage, circumstance, strengths, weaknesses and achievements—is made of the same kinds of cells, doing the same jobs. Everyone has stem cells, muscle cells and bone cells. We are all, genetically speaking at least, more than 99.9 per cent identical.

Just think about that for a minute. Picture someone you love or admire and then consider the fact that you are 99.9 per cent genetically identical to them. How does that make you feel? It's quite an intimate feeling isn't it?

Now, think about a random city in a country you've never visited before. Conjure a simple image of someone who lives there—a stranger you will never meet, whose life looks very different from yours, whose concerns and joys are not the same, who, from the outside at least, has very little in common with you. Now consider that you are also 99.9 per cent genetically identical to each other. For that matter, you and I are 99.9 per cent genetically identical.

Any time I consider this, I feel closer to people and am reminded that we're all human, we all inhabit the same planet. We're all a wild combination of trillions of cells and a soul, just moving through space and time, reacting to situations and making choices. How does that idea make you feel? Connected? Overwhelmed? Fearful? If so, that, right there, is awe.

Now, take a moment to consider your breath. The constancy of it. Think about how it's the soundtrack of our lives, always with us, mostly ignored, so familiar as to disappear from our awareness altogether, the very epitome of being taken for granted.

Now consider that as an average adult at rest you will breathe approximately sixteen times per minute, which means you'll take around 960 breaths every hour, 23,040 a day, or 8,409,600 each year.

If you live to be 80 years old, you will take approximately 672,768,000 breaths over your lifetime. In and out. Every day. Sleeping or awake. Delighted or morose. Healthy or unwell. This simple act of breathing invokes both awe and fear when you think about how utterly vital and complex it is, and how little we pay attention to it.

When you draw a breath in through your mouth, the air is pulled down your trachea, where it funnels into two tubes called bronchi. One of these leads to the left lung, the other to the right. These bronchi then divide into successively smaller and smaller tubes, like the branches of a tree, getting finer as they reach down into your lungs. The smallest of these tubes are called bronchioles and are as thin as a single strand of hair. Each of your lungs has around 30,000 bronchioles, at the end of which you'll find tiny air sacs called alveoli. You have about 600 million alveoli in your lungs, each of which has incredibly thin cell walls (approximately 0.0001 centimetres) that allow the oxygen you breathe in to pass directly to your red blood cells and keep your body fuelled so it can continue to function. This process happens every time you inhale.

This process then reverses (CO_2—alveoli—bronchiole—bronchi—trachea—mouth) as you exhale. Sixteen times per minute. 23,000 times a day. More than 8 million times a year.

Picking up your Time-bending tool for a moment, take some time now to draw a deep breath down into your lungs and picture this process unfolding as you do so. Feel your chest expand and your belly push out as you picture the air going down your throat, all the way through your bronchi and bronchioles, until it reaches the alveoli and the oxygen hits your bloodstream. Then, as your chest drops and you exhale, picture the CO_2 travelling back through the same pathways. Ridding your body of carbon dioxide as you breathe out.

Before you put your Time-bending tool away, think for a moment about your heart—another amazingly complex part of your body that works without rest. Another process we're barely aware of unless something changes or goes wrong, yet whether we pay attention or not, it's there, keeping us alive.

Your incredible heart beats approximately 80 times per minute, 4800 times an hour, 115,000 times a day, 42 million times a year, or more than 3 billion times over the course of an average lifetime.

Next time you're lying with someone you love (it might be a person or animal, or even your own beautiful self), place your hand over their heart and lie still. Quietly bring your attention to the beating of their heart under your hand. Focus on the persistence and rhythm of this powerful marker of life, love, existence and a shared moment in time. Consider how grateful you are to that muscle, for pumping blood around their body, for keeping them alive, for allowing you to share space with them, to share love with them. It's a pretty incredible experience.

All of our bodies do these things. Some better than others, some for longer than others, but we all breathe, we all have heartbeats, we all rely on the same processes from the same 37 trillion cells, and we're all in the messiness and miracle of life together.

The reason I'm so enamoured with the quantifiable—the number of breaths and the frequency of heartbeats—is that putting a figure on them makes something that feels infinite seem precious. If our breath and heartbeat offer a benefit other than keeping us alive, it's the reminder that every one of them counts. That my life and all the beauty and wonder and awe it brings me is not infinite. It will end one day. Every breath matters, every moment is important. Every pain and joy will pass.

If you take on board no other experiments from this chapter, I'd encourage you to spend one minute every day just thinking about the incredible creation that is your body. Set a reminder in your calendar every day for a week or do it every time you make a cup of tea. Notice how your perception changes and whether thinking about your body leads to a heightened awareness of the tiny, awe-inducing parts of your everyday life.

Your brain

Our brains are truly incredible. Not only do we breathe, sit, read, blink, work, love, parent, support, touch and feel using our brains, but our brains are also where our essence lives. Any time you've solved a difficult problem, any time you've created something, any time you've grappled with difficult emotions and come to an understanding, any time you've lived with a mental illness, chosen forgiveness or kindness or laughter or gentleness—that's you: that's your brain.

The brain is mysterious and phenomenal in so many ways. For example, did you know that the blood vessels in your brain alone measure more than 600 kilometres long? Or that when we fall in love, the heightened sense of joy, pleasure and lightness we feel is a physiological reaction where parts of the brain associated with pleasure and reward become activated. Did you know that the brainwaves of two musicians can actually synchronise when performing together? Or that your brain generates approximately 50,000 thoughts per day?

unlock the awe and wonder
of the world

I love thinking about the brains of my favourite creators and the fact that all their output—their music or poetry or books or paintings or performances or designs or buildings or inventions—have originated from one single brain. Margaret Atwood, for example, has published more than 60 books of poetry, fiction, short stories and non-fiction, many of which have made their way into popular culture and into our discussions on gender, politics, religion and climate change. In some instances, her work has actually become emblematic of these issues on a global scale. And it all originated from one brain. I'm similarly amazed by the brains of Jane Campion and Maya Angelou and Thelma Plum and countless others whose ideas set in motion waves that continue to reach further out into the world, changing hearts, connecting minds and breathing life into ideas.

Child-like wonder

Think back to when you were a child, when joy and discovery and wonder were your reality rather than a bittersweet nostalgia. What do you remember?

I remember spending hours looking through the wrong end of binoculars, studying the up-close structure of everyday things: how the denim of my jeans looked like the indigo peaks and valleys of an alien planet; how a sprinkling of sand in my palm became a field of boulders and how the bark of trees became canyons and peaks.

These experiences of wonder are not lost to you as an adult. Using a basic schoolkids' microscope or by inverting a pair of binoculars, you can study a spoonful of soil from the garden or take a closer look at what sludgy creatures exist in the birdbath water.

You can also think like a child and unlock the awe and wonder of the world by pulling out your Not-knowing magnifying glass and simply asking questions and then being curious enough to search out the answers.

Why do bees make a buzzing sound?

How does a seed know when to grow?

What makes laughter contagious?

Where do our memories live?

Why *is* the sky blue?

None of this is about reverting to childish behaviours, dragging your feet or asking 'Why?' so often that you drive your friends to distraction. It's about reclaiming wonder, finding awe in the tiniest of moments and choosing to take time in which to do it. When you find yourself in the company of an inquisitive child, instead of viewing their constant questioning as an inconvenience, accept the invitation to join them in their wonder. In our busy lives, what we stand to gain when we slow down and look a little closer, even for a few seconds, is worth the time it takes.

Tiny and vast

Consider now, for just a minute, the tiniest of tiny wonders that surround us. Those we can't even see. The molecules in a drop of water, the number of atoms in a breath of air, the unseen forces that help a seed to germinate. Not only does nature not need to be big to be awe-inspiring, it doesn't even need to be visible.

Imagine a drop of water in the palm of your hand. Think of how insignificant it is, how you would wipe it on the leg of your pants without a second thought. Scientists estimate that this standard, everyday drop contains more than 1.5 sextillion molecules.

You might be surprised to learn that a sextillion is, in fact, a real number (I know I was) and that it is the equivalent of a billion trillions. If you start with a one and follow it with twenty-one zeroes, you have a sextillion.

To give some context to just how big a number that is, it would take Earth's current population of 7.5 billion people more than 28,000 years to collectively speak a sextillion words, and given that our population is the largest it ever has been, more than doubling in the last fifty years, it's safe to say that the entirety of the human race has not yet uttered its sextillionth word.

Put another way, if you stacked a sextillion people in a tower, one on top of the next, it would be 180,000 light years tall (taller than the diameter of our entire Milky Way galaxy).

And yet, there are 1.5 sextillion molecules in a single drop of water, just resting in the palm of your hand.

Have you ever wondered which there is more of—grains of sand on all the beaches in the world, or stars in the universe?

A study run by the University of Hawaii set out to answer the first part of the question by calculating how many grains of sand are on all of Earth's beaches. Turns out there's a lot. Like, a mind-bending amount. Seven quintillion, five quadrillion grains of sand. That's a 75 followed by 17 zeroes.

Also a lot is the number of stars in our Milky Way galaxy, which NASA estimates at around 100 billion. If we then assume that the 10 billion other galaxies in the observable universe also have approximately 100 billion stars each, that means there are roughly a sextillion (1 billion trillion) stars in the observable universe. Again, that's a one with twenty-one zeroes—a number much, much larger than the total number of grains of sand on Earth.

Next time you're on a beach, try to fathom this vastness. It's challenging to contemplate, particularly when you return to the drop of water we began with, with its 1.5 sextillion molecules. When I realise that I can hold more molecules in my hand than there are stars in the universe, it strikes me that vastness can be seen up close just as much as it can be seen from far away, a fact I find simultaneously awe-inspiring and, quite frankly, terrifying.

It's the same feeling I get when I lie on the ground at night, watching the stars gradually make their way across the sky, the occasional shooting star crossing the dome of deepest blue. When I allow my mind to open up to the enormity and brain-twisting vastness of the infinite universe and our tiny, infinitesimal presence—only for a half second, as though I know any longer will expose me to ideas and truths that will melt my mind. When my head swims with the marvel and terror of it all, aware for a brief moment, as my stomach loops and drops and I find myself clinging to the ground in the half-formed fear that letting go would see me float up into the heavens, untethered.

That's awe.

If, like me, you find these thoughts overwhelming or even out-right scary, it might help to keep this in mind: one very important distinction between awe and other related emotions such as inspiration or surprise is that it has the tendency to make us feel small. While our human egos may struggle with that, this is actually where the power of awe lies: it forces us to look beyond our own problems, our own part of the world and the events that impact us directly. Awe makes us see ourselves as a small piece of something much, much larger. This self-diminishment makes us feel humbled, which in turn means that we are less likely to demonstrate selfish tendencies such as entitlement, arrogance and narcissism. Feeling humbled and connected also makes us *want* to reach out and engage with others—all of which, as we know, is important for our own wellbeing and the wellbeing of our families, friendship groups, neighbourhoods, communities, cities and countries.

This is actually where
the power of awe lies:
it forces us to look beyond
our own problems, our
own part of the world
and the events that impact
us directly. Awe makes
us see ourselves as a
small piece of something
much, much larger.

The natural world

Our exploration of awe was always going to end up back here—at glittering waterfalls and caves lit by glow-worms and the raging audacity of bushfire, and while the next chapter is dedicated to the benefits of spending time in nature, the opportunities for awe in our natural world are too plentiful not to mention here.

The good news for the time-poor and stressed-out among us is that the natural experience doesn't need to be grand in order for us to benefit. There's no need to climb a mountain or kayak rapids, because it turns out that even the simplest moments outdoors deliver the same advantages.

Nature exists along a spectrum of impressiveness, from the humdrum of ants hurriedly going about their efficiencies to the ferocity of a great white shark breaching the surface of the ocean.

Nature also exists on a spectrum of size, from the microscopic plankton in our oceans to the great baleen whales that feed on them, from a pocket park in your inner-city neighbourhood to the remoteness of the Northeast Greenland National Park—the world's largest national park, measuring over 970,000 square kilometres.

Spending time in nature—hiking; skiing; bushwalking; stargazing; gardening; surfing; snorkelling; ice skating on a frozen lake; sitting still on a spongy, damp, fallen tree and watching the bush come alive in the stillness; observing a bird's nest over months, from construction to eggs to constant vigilance and hatching, feeding and insistent pink beaks pleading for food, to fluffy heads, learning to fly and finally moving on—offers experiences that will change your life if you allow them to. Simply by taking time and bending it as we spend a few moments in the noticing and the awe of them.

Tiny and vast and everything in between, nature is all around us, within and without. The potential for experiencing awe is everywhere too.

IF YOU HAVE HALF A MINUTE

- Place your fingers over the strongest pulse in your body and sit quietly as you pay attention to its constant thrum.

- Pause outside for a moment one night and look up at the stars.

- Look at photos or videos from an awe-inspiring experience you've had.

- Think back to a time you've experienced awe and tap back into those memories.

- Consider this: nerve impulses can travel to and from the brain at speeds of over 400 km/hour.

- And this: Earth is currently spinning at approximately 1600 km/hour—we just can't feel it.

- Think about your lungs, your heart, your brain and the incredible ways in which they work without you needing to pay attention to them.

- Before you take a bite of your apple, take a moment to wonder where it came from, how long it took to grow, how it got from farm to supermarket to your hand.

IF YOU HAVE HALF AN HOUR

- Go for a brisk walk and then stand still, focusing on the sensation of your blood moving through your body.

- Read an article—or start reading a book—about a person you admire.

- Create an awe playlist full of music that inspires you or fills you with wonder.

- Visit a lookout and see how the earth unfolds below you like a patchwork quilt, or see if you can spot the gentle curve of the horizon.

- Go for a wonder walk in your garden or a park and move at a snail's pace—one step every thirty seconds.

- Ask a friend about their own awe-inspiring experiences.

- Visit a local cemetery and spend time thinking about the lives of all the people buried there.

- Write a journal entry about an awe experience you've previously had.

- Grab a magnifying glass, microscope or a trusty pair of binoculars used backwards, and spend time looking at things like paper, grass, water and rocks.

- Find some soil to dig in and look for worms.

- Lie next to someone you love and place your hand on their chest—feeling the beat of their heart.

IF YOU HAVE HALF A DAY OR MORE

- Go for a hike and instead of listening to music or a podcast, focus on the sensations of filling and emptying your lungs with every breath.

- Visit a museum or gallery and marvel at the brainwork of others.

- Think of things you loved doing as a child and try doing them again (maybe finger painting, climbing trees or watching butterflies).

- Go for a moonwalk one night and look at how the moon paints your neighbourhood silver.

- Spend time creating an awe-inspiration collection with photos, videos, articles and reminders of awe experiences you've had—dip into it as needed.

- Watch a documentary about a person, place or feat that inspires you (check out *Period. End of Sentence.*, *RBG* or *The Final Quarter* if you don't know where to start).

CHAPTER 4

nature

Wild dill and radish

cling to the edge of the road

The plaintive cry of a black cockatoo,

backlit by the hovering sun

Bruised thunderheads,

the air crackles—a living thing—

as colonies of cicadas chorus

coarse as a river crashing on rocks below

Feathers aloft in the damp updraft

and raindrops like gold come suddenly,

seeping slowly into soil,

into valleys and caverns and creeks.

And my chest fills,

my blood pumps

my eyes see

my body trembles

my chest empties.

Over, and over

And over.

The rain falls and the sun bakes

as the wild dill and radish

cling to the edge of the road,

humming with life.

I grew up in a household that valued time outside.

My family went camping, we would have picnics and eat outside on warm summer nights, alternating our time between the outdoor table and the pool. On any occasion when I complained of being bored, I was sent outside to find something interesting to do—and can I tell you, it was very annoying that I would always find it.

In spite of growing up with a solid foundation in the outdoors, as I got older and became a full-time-employed adult, the hours I spent outside diminished quickly. I spent my workdays waking before sunrise, driving to the train station, sitting on a train for an hour before transferring to a bus for another twenty minutes. I'd then walk across a soccer field to my office, where I'd sit at my desk, staring at a screen or talking on the phone, comfortable in the climate-controlled environment of steel and concrete and glass. I would get to the end of my workday and do the reverse commute home, where I'd eat dinner, watch TV, go to bed and do it all again the next day.

I'd have maybe thirty minutes outside each workday, with the rest of my time spent indoors, the air sweetly conditioned and my desk fluorescently lit. Often I was outside a little more on weekends, but I'd approximate that I spent less than 10 per cent of my life outdoors, and probably only 1 per cent intentionally so.

I'd like to tell you that this changed as I matured, but that would be a lie. Even as I moved out of my parents' house, got married, bought a home of my own and became a parent myself, I spent the vast majority of my time indoors, leaving the house to go for a quick walk around the block, to get into my car, to hang the laundry or to check the mail. I'd convinced myself that, as a business owner, as a parent, as the partner of someone who left the house before the sun came up and came home after our daughter was in bed, I simply didn't have time to spend outside.

It was the most disconnected I've ever been from nature and it's no surprise that this is also the period of my life where I developed crippling anxiety and severe postnatal depression. I'm not going to suggest that I would have avoided mental illness had I spent more time outdoors, but I will say that I wish I had listened to my intuition, which was telling me that I needed to get out into nature, to get my hands in the soil, to grow something, to reconnect with the natural world. I knew this because I constantly had a stack of gardening books on my bedside table and a notepad filled with half-finished sketches of the veggie plot I dreamt of creating in our backyard. I knew all about what to plant, where to plant it and why to rotate crops. I was primed to get outside and get digging. Instead of just doing it, though, I turned to the blue-lit oblivion offered by my phone and developed a quite frankly ridiculous addiction to a game called Hay Day—an agriculture-simulation game that 'lets you get back to nature and experience the simple life of working the land'. The irony is not lost on me, dear reader.

In case you're wondering: yes, Hay Day is exactly what it sounds like—an online game where I could pretend to be a farmer, growing and harvesting digital crops.

Yes, I was an adult at this time.

Yes, I'm a bit embarrassed to admit it.

No, actually, I wasn't alone in this addiction. It turns out that Hay Day was hugely popular, with millions of players logging on, digging in, planting out and harvesting their imaginary crops every day.

I mean, if I woke up with my head stapled to a tree and a note telling me to 'Go for a bushwalk now', tied around my neck, it couldn't have been any clearer that I needed to get outside. The only problem was that I wasn't paying attention to signs. I was too busy with pretend crop rotation (unnecessarily so, can I add, as it made no difference to the composition of the virtual soil or the outcome of the game), hovering over my phone, waiting to harvest my apples.

One night as I watched my soybean crop inch towards readiness, when I should have been asleep, the utter absurdity of the situation finally hit me. I was obviously craving the experience of growing something, getting my hands in the dirt and reconnecting to the natural world, but had instead chosen this digital stand-in. The big question was: why?

First, playing farmer on my phone was risk-free and easy. There were no caterpillars or snails that would munch on my seedlings, no extreme heat or frost to contend with. Secondly, I was assured a positive result from minimum effort (if result meant nothing more tangible than Hay Day currency and access to new crop types— blueberries, here I come). No matter how lacklustre my input, this digital version of nature would provide for me what I felt entitled to.

There lies the central issue of our disconnection with nature today. In Western culture, we see ourselves as the dominant intelligent force that has, in many ways, learnt to conquer nature. We want it to serve us and provide us with the things we need from it, as well as the things we want. At the same time, we want it to be controllable and manageable, or at least predictable. We feel entitled to that because we are quite obviously the governing force, with our machines and buildings and concrete and zoning laws. Take that, nature, you big pushover!

Even the way we speak about nature offers clues as to how we see her. We talk about 'spending time in nature' as if it's separate from us—a somewhere and something else. A fenced-in parcel of land we visit on occasion, wrapped up inside our national parks or the boundary fences of designated wilderness.

Since the industrial revolution we've done a tremendous job
of separating ourselves from the natural world and consistently
worked to wrangle it into submission. The 1950s, with its explosion
of gadgetry and convenience, brought about a steep decline in
our time spent outdoors, and cemented the belief that all of our
innovations have made us the biggest and most assertive influence
on the planet. We've since convinced ourselves, as tech has gotten
more ubiquitous and all-encompassing, that our civilisation sets
us apart, that buildings and transport and air conditioning and
the internet mean that we're ranked above the natural world. As
though the air we breathe isn't created by trees and the ocean.
As though the fruits and vegetables we eat aren't grown on plants
fed by the sun, rooted in the soil. As though the lakes and rivers
and rainclouds don't provide us with water to drink.

If the natural world could, and did, disappear—oceans empty,
animals gone, trees turned to dust and blown away—how long do
you think we'd last? Estimates suggest there'd be enough oxygen
in the atmosphere to support human life for anywhere from 100 to
1200 years. But when you also remove water and food, the estimates
dwindle dramatically. We'd survive weeks, maybe, months at best,
if our reserves of stored food and water stretched that far. Some
people like to think we're independent of nature, but the truth is
we can't survive without it.

The natural world, on the other hand, would be perfectly
fine if humans disappeared tomorrow. There would be a messy
reclamation of the previously held human spaces, as the towns and
cities and highways reverted to nature, but over time the natural
world would not only survive and heal, it would thrive without us.

As much as our human egos might insist otherwise, people depend
on nature. We are nature. Our bodies are ecosystems in themselves
and we are part of larger ecosystems. Nature is not here to simply

We talk about
'spending time in
nature' as if it's
separate from
us—a somewhere
and something else.

serve us, to be cut down, used up, paved over and forgotten on our way to expanding civilisation or profitability.

For every hour the average Australian spends outdoors, we now spend more than seven inside on a screen, and according to research conducted by Planet Ark, one in three of us spends less than eighteen minutes a day outdoors. Since the 1990s, Australian backyards have been shrinking as homes get larger and blocks get smaller. The same research surveyed more than 1000 Australian parents and found that only one in five children climbs trees, while more than a third have never gone camping. Areas of untouched wilderness are disappearing at an astonishing rate, with more than three-quarters of land in the world no longer considered wild. The situation is even worse for our oceans, where the only areas left untouched by industrial fishing, pollution and shipping are almost completely confined to the polar regions.

And yet, despite our growing disconnection from it, on some deep level many of us understand how important it is to spend time in nature. We will travel to the ocean to swim in the salt water, or walk to the end of a pier only to stare at the expanse stretching out before us, to draw the briny air into our lungs. We will find and ascend the highest hill or structure we can simply to scan the horizon for a silver ribbon of river or a blue smear of far-off mountains. We will seek out clean air or tall trees or waterfalls and stand close to them, breathing in the compounds and ions and chemicals they each provide. We might not understand how or why, but we know that it makes us feel better.

Nature has power over us and, in spite of the modern conveniences we've created in order to try to tame her, to manage and control and predict her, we are still drawn to her wildness.

It's no surprise, really. The science behind spending time in nature is phenomenal. So much so that GPs in parts of the United Kingdom have begun prescribing time in nature as a complementary therapy to patients trying to reduce their risk of heart disease and stroke, as well as those looking to improve their mental health and overall wellbeing.

Unfortunately, like many other worthy wellness ideas that become mainstream, there's been an increase in the commercialisation of 'time in nature' over the past few years, as entrepreneurs commodify what should be an accessible experience for everyone, wrap it up in expensive technical gear or market it towards the corporate sector. We read books about the healing power of trees, listen to podcasts about rewilding, research the benefits of spending more time in natural places and then, so used to solutions this powerful costing us money, we look for a product that will deliver the benefits to us: retreats and coaching programs and head-office-mandated bonding sessions spent in canoes, or multiday hikes and epic, once-in-a-lifetime wilderness experiences that we pay big bucks for. Suddenly we need a consultant to show us the most effective way to engage with nature so that we can then return to our climate-controlled workplaces, restored and rejuvenated and ready to kick corporate goals once more.

While there is undoubtedly a huge amount to be gained from forest bathing for a few hours, going off-grid camping for a weekend or hiking the Larapinta Trail for two weeks, I want to redefine what 'spending time in nature' can look like and hopefully open you up to a whole world of Small Care regardless of where you live, how much time you have and whether you've got the gear or not.

This brings me to ask two questions: what even is nature? And what happens when we spend time immersed in it?

When asked to picture nature I used to imagine shimmering lakes and pristine grasslands and forests stretching as far as the eye could see. I'd imagine lions stalking across savannahs, koalas gazing down sleepily from high up in a gum tree and eagles soaring on thermals hundreds of metres above the ground. In other words, I pictured experiences that are not everyday options for the vast majority of us. Perhaps experiences that are once or twice in a lifetime for most. It wasn't until I read Florence Williams' book *The Nature Fix* and discovered Oscar Wilde's definition of nature as a 'place where birds fly around uncooked' that I really loosened my grip on what nature could be and, as a result, found a definition that feels inclusive and accessible.

Yes, nature is waterfalls and grasslands and untouched wilderness, but it can also be your own backyard, a community garden, the school playground, the tiny park you walk through on your way home every night. It can be the trees planted up and down your street or a pot of flowers on your balcony. Nature is always present—it's the air in your lungs and the water in your glass and the pear sitting on your desk.

Trees: a love story

I've come a long way since my Hay Day period. After my epiphany I deleted the app and began what can only be described as my own personal Nature 101 course. What started as spending one minute in my garden every morning, inspecting the plants and flowers, noticing the seasonal comings and goings of birds and insects, the changing light and shadows, has gradually become an enduring love affair with the natural world—trees and forests in particular.

Now I have a ponderosa pine tattooed on my inner upper arm, a forever reminder of the importance of trees, and the healing and wisdom they offer us—if only we choose to look closely enough.

There are so many tree facts I've learnt over the years that fill me with unbelievable joy. For example, did you know that some species of trees can communicate through an underground network of soil fungi that connects individual trees to each other and allows them to share carbon, water and information about drought and other threats? Did you know that they can pass chemical signals to each other, warning nearby trees of impending insect attack and compelling them to produce more insect-resistant chemicals as protection?

My favourite, however, is the magic of phytoncides. Certain types of trees and plants produce chemical compounds called phytoncides: the natural oils that are a vital part of the tree's defence system. They emit these phytoncides in order to protect themselves from bacteria, insects and fungal attacks, and to alert surrounding trees to a potential threat. They can dial the production of these oils up or down as needed. In other words, phytoncides are one of the ways trees 'talk' to and look after each other. What's more, when you or I happen to walk past them or breathe in their oils, we also benefit from these potent chemical compounds.

Exposure to phytoncides has been found to significantly decrease our levels of stress hormones, as well as reduce feelings of anxiety, anger and fatigue. They can also lower blood pressure, while improving both the quality and number of hours we sleep. Phytoncides support our parasympathetic nervous system and reduce the 'fight or flight' sensation we can experience when stressed or agitated—all of which is compelling—but even more important is the impact phytoncides have on our 'natural killer' cells. These cells are part of our immune system and kill tumour cells or cells that are infected with a virus. They're essential for a healthy immune system, and exposure to phytoncides has been shown to not only significantly increase the number of natural killer cells in the body, but also enhance the activity of several anti-cancer proteins. What's more, this effect can last for more than thirty days after exposure to phytoncides.

About 40 years ago, someone planted a huge stand of California redwoods on a vacant piece of land in our town. They've grown to be giants, at least 30 metres high, and once you walk under their canopy, the rest of the world disappears. The ground is spongy with fallen needles and the air is soft, filled with piney scent and muffled birdsong. There are wombat burrows dotted throughout and a handful of different tracks wind down the hill. I try to walk in these trees every day and every time I do, regardless of what stress or tension I'm carrying with me, ten minutes among the trees makes me feel better. Calmer, lighter and better equipped to face the rest of the day. It feels a lot like melting—into a place, and into a calmer version of myself. I've started calling it 'tree medicine'.

In his beautiful book *Forest Bathing: How Trees Can Help You Find Health and Happiness*, Dr Qing Li further convinced me that this feeling of wellbeing wasn't just something fanciful. He shares incredible evidence of the healing power of time in the trees but, even more importantly, describes why forest bathing (known as *shinrin-yoku* in Japanese) is so vital to developing our connection with nature:

> This is more than just a walk . . . *shinrin-yoku* means taking in the forest through our senses. This is not exercise. It is simply being in nature, connecting with it through our sense of sight, hearing, taste, smell and touch. Indoors, we tend to use only two senses, our eyes and our ears. Outside is where we can smell the flowers, taste the fresh air, look at the changing colours of the trees, hear the birds singing and feel the breeze on our skin. And when we open up our senses, we begin to connect with the natural world.

It's when we tap into this deep connection with the natural world that we can see not only our place in it, and the role we have in caring for it, but also the ways in which the natural world cares right back. Trees take the CO_2 we exhale (not to mention the CO_2 our civilisation produces) and turn it into the oxygen we need to breathe. They provide us with shelter and protection, they soothe our stresses, they offer habitat to animals and insects that are vital to our survival, they cool Earth, repair the soil and provide a place of refuge. The impact that fans out from time spent in the trees is phenomenal, and all they ask in return is that we don't cut them down, that we care for our shared home.

Get that vitamin tree

On some elemental level, with or without scientific evidence, we understand that spending time in nature is good for us. We can see it in our own behaviours and moods, and if you have young kids you probably know all too well the crotchety, cranky agitation that comes when they've had too much screen time or been indoors for too long. Lockdown was a stark reminder of the draw of nature too, as we were pulled to our gardens, hands in the dirt, heads in the sun, or we craved the outdoors like oxygen itself, which meant that those first days of eased restrictions were spent in the sun: on the beach, in the surf or on the trails, visiting gardens and parks and playgrounds. We all promised never to take time in nature for granted again.

Of course, time has a way of fading such promises, like a piece of fabric left too long in the sun, leaving it bleached and ghostly. Many of us, in the time since our various lockdowns ended, have reverted back to our previously distant relationship with nature.

To convince you to reconsider, I'd love to simply say that time in nature is good for us and for that to be enough. That we would all happily find twenty minutes a day or two hours on the weekend to immerse ourselves in nature and let the positive benefits roll in.

We understand that
spending time in
nature is good for us.
We can see it in our
own behaviours
and moods.

But just because we know something is good for us doesn't mean we do it. We know kale is good for us, but does that mean we all joyfully eat it every day? Beyond our deeply held but often-ignored intuition that yes, time in nature is good for us, what specific effects does it have? Decades of research shows us that time in nature can:

- decrease anxiety levels
- improve mood
- supplement existing clinical treatments for people with major depressive disorders
- improve self-esteem, particularly in people who are predisposed to depression and anxiety
- restore our attention and focus
- improve creative thinking and problem-solving abilities
- reduce the impact of mental fatigue
- result in higher job satisfaction
- improve short-term memory function
- reduce symptoms of stress
- reduce cortisol levels
- result in improved overall health and reduced early mortality
- increase happiness
- improve sleep quality and duration
- lower blood pressure
- improve vision and reduce the chance of developing myopia (nearsightedness), particularly in children (I know this one sounds unlikely, but there is evidence going back to Dr Kathryn Rose's 2008 opthalmology study that shows more time outside

and less time spent on 'near work' results in better
vision and reduced likelihood of myopia in children)

- **reduce inflammation**
- reduce cancer risk by increasing natural killer cells
  and cancer-fighting proteins
- **reduce the risk of developing type 2 diabetes**
- strengthen the immune system
- **reduce the risk of cardiovascular disease**
- increase our love of natural places and the likelihood
  that we will act to protect them.

There's no denying that these benefits are powerful and could have
enormous impacts on our individual health, wellbeing (mental and
physical) and performance, and an even more significant impact if
you look at the ripple effects of these improvements. Widespread
time in nature could mean healthier citizens who require less
medication and less medical intervention in their lives; workplaces
where employees are mentally refreshed and more satisfied in their
roles; and societies full of creative thinkers and problem-solvers
and nature-lovers who do everything they can to protect the natural
world they love.

The next question is: how? If we really are disconnected from
nature, working longer hours, spending more time indoors, how
can we reconnect?

I'm stuck indoors

Let's get the elephant in the room front and centre, straightaway.
There are situations where you cannot avoid being indoors for
lengthy periods of time. Maybe it's work-related—nurses typically
can't treat patients outdoors, for example—or perhaps air pollution

or extreme weather keeps you indoors. Maybe you have mobility or health issues that keep you confined or maybe (and this is purely hypothetical of course) you're on a book deadline and have welded yourself to your seat.

None of those reasons mean that the benefits of the natural world are out of your reach. There's a surprisingly significant number of things you can do to access nature's calming and healing superpowers even while you're stuck inside.

Essential oils

Before you roll your eyes thinking I'm about to dive into some of the more spurious claims of the multibillion-dollar essential oils wellness industry (no, your essential-oil blend is not going to cure Covid-19, Ebola or ADHD for that matter), hold the phone for a sec.

We've already covered the research into phytoncides and the positive impact they can have on our health; other research from Dr Qing Li shows that even being exposed to the diffused essential oils of some of the most prolific phytoncide producers (think cedar, pine and hinoki cypress) offers many of the same benefits as wandering through a forest of these trees. In fact, when stressed-out staff in a Vanderbilt University Medical Center ward began diffusing these kinds of essential oils in their workplace, they experienced some pretty incredible results. Before they began using the essential oils, 41 per cent of staff experienced work-related stress frequently, but this dropped to only 3 per cent after the oils were diffused. At the same time, their perceived energy levels rose from 33 per cent to 77 per cent. While originally just 13 per cent of staff felt well equipped to handle stressful work situations, by the end of the experiment that had risen to 58 per cent. Further studies have found that breathing in the vaporised oils of some of these trees activates the same physiological responses as walking among them.

To try it out yourself, you could bring a diffuser into your office, or put a few drops of oil on a handkerchief or the pulse points of your wrist and neck to smell throughout the day.

Indoor plants

Long championed for their air-purifying qualities, it turns out that growing plants indoors has other positive benefits too. Even if there's next to no natural light available, you'll find an indoor plant to suit your home or office. There, you can watch it grow and experience a genuine sense of anticipation and joy any time you notice the unfurling of a new leaf. It may seem like a small thing but watching this process, noticing your plant swivel towards the light during the day or seeing its flower buds form over time, offers you an up-close connection to nature and a real-time view of the miracle of life.

Growing indoor plants should come with a warning though—you will probably find that one is never enough. There is something truly wondrous about them and even the most avid brown thumb can find themselves transformed by growing a plant or two (or thirty).

Any green (view) will do

Believe it or not, you can access a lot of the benefits of nature even on the days you can't leave the office or if sick kids have you stuck inside. Simply looking out your window to some kind of greenery (trees, grass, parks, even a window box with some flowers), spending a minute or two looking at nature videos or images on your phone, listening to nature sounds or having a green wall in view all have a significant impact on our wellbeing.

In a 2015 *Journal of Environmental Psychology* study, Australian researchers discovered that looking at either a computerised image of green rooftops or the real deal for as little as 40 seconds can significantly improve your attention and provide a restorative mental break during the workday, while looking at the colour green (even if it's just a brief glimpse of a green wall) is potent enough to help increase our creative performance. Even listening to recordings of nature sounds, such as birdsong, a rushing creek or wind through the leaves, has a restorative cognitive effect, makes us more productive and helps us to feel more positive about our work environment.

All of this means that, no matter how much time you spend indoors, you're able to access some of the immediate benefits of nature. You could create a gallery of nature images and videos on your phone or take photos of wildflowers you spot when you're out walking and spend a few minutes of your lunchbreak looking through them. A change as small as swapping your phone screensaver or desktop wallpaper to a photo from one of your nature expeditions can also have a positive impact, providing you with a nature-themed touchstone throughout the day. Similarly, you can put a photo on your desk of your favourite wild place, tree, river or park and spend a moment looking at it each morning. I know these seem like insignificant acts, almost childlike, but there is genuine power in surrounding yourself with nature, and since many of us are often deficient in exposure, even the briefest of nature interludes is powerful.

Nature is literally everywhere

Nature is in us and around us, in spite of our attempts to pretend otherwise as we seal ourselves in our climate-controlled office towers, commute in our climate-controlled vehicles and return to our climate-controlled homes.

Trees get a lot of love (and rightly so) for providing us with the oxygen we breathe, but according to the National Ocean Service, it's our oceans that are the planet's true superheroes, responsible for producing more than 50 per cent of the oxygen we breathe. No matter where in the world you live, how far away from the ocean you are, of every ten breaths you take, at least five of them are of oxygen produced by the ocean. More specifically, the oxygen is produced by the algae and microorganisms called phytoplankton that live in the ocean, which take carbon dioxide and turn it into the air we breathe.

Meanwhile, the fresh food we are all reliant on depends on the most underrated of essentials: soil. A single handful of healthy soil can contain up to 50 *billion* microorganisms, and while we cannot see them with our naked eye, these microorganisms are essential to building productive soils and therefore essential to life on Earth. If we have no healthy soil, then plants and trees will fail to thrive. If there are no plants and trees, then there will soon be no pollinators, no flowers, no fruits, no vegetables or grains or nuts—nothing to sustain us or the other animals that rely on the same plants to survive.

How can we ever look at the soil underfoot as mere dirt when we know how important it is, once we recognise that one *handful* is far, far more populated by microorganisms than our entire planet is by humans? Every crunchy carrot, every sweet slice of watermelon, every summer-grown tomato has come from the soil and been fuelled by the sun.

If you're stuck indoors most of the day, or even if you don't feel that you have regular access to nature, I can almost guarantee that at some stage in your day you will walk past or across a patch of soil—maybe it's a little nature strip on the way to the bus stop or a garden across from your office. This everyday-bordering-on-insignificant moment offers you the opportunity to be awed by the teeming population of microbes underfoot.

You probably don't need to look far to see just how tenacious life can be. Yes, it's true that the fragile ecosystems on Earth require balance, care and protection from humans, but there are always instances of the perseverance of life if you're willing to look for them—a rooftop falcon's nest, a stand of jacaranda trees flowering madly in the middle of a busy city road, wildflowers thriving on the edge of train tracks. As Jeff Goldblum famously said in *Jurassic Park*, life finds a way, so consider this your daily invitation to pick up your Not-knowing tool, take a moment and look for evidence of it.

Okay, I'm outdoors, now what?

Now we get to claim our spot in the natural neighbourhood that surrounds us. The green spaces near your work, home and school, the trails you ride, the local nature reserve, the beaches you visit, the mountains you climb or the hills you ski down—these places are your natural neighbourhood, and whether you're someone who already values time in nature, someone who wants to find more of it or someone looking to start, we need to become accustomed to noticing the natural world that's already part of our daily lives.

Once we begin taking time to notice what's around us, we begin to view ourselves not as a separate entity, a visitor or an outsider, but as a small part of the fabric of the place, no more or less important than any other. It's from this feeling of belonging that we might discover a sense of responsibility for a place, a need to advocate for our natural neighbourhoods and all they entail. We might recognise in ourselves a previously undiscovered, but deeply held, desire to take care of and ensure the protection of this place. I believe that we're only going to do that if we truly care about it. And the best way to learn to care is to start noticing.

Find a sit spot

A sit spot is exactly what it sounds like: A spot. To sit. In nature.

Try to find somewhere with a green outlook that you're likely to be able to visit easily. This probably means a place that's close to home, school or work. Once you're there, take a moment to find a comfortable position—it might be on a bench, a smooth patch of ground with your back against the trunk of a tree, or a flat rock overlooking a lake—then just sit, and observe. Even if this feels strange, resist the temptation to pull out your phone (or better yet, leave it behind). Allow yourself to acknowledge the strangeness but don't let it pull you away from your noticing.

As you sit, learn to watch the comings and goings around you. The insects that crawl and fly and work ceaselessly. The bees and spiders and butterflies. Notice the many different shades of green, the bursts of colour from flowers and plants, the birdsong and the breeze in the leaves. Just soak in the detail and right-pacedness of the natural world and consider this: there are no clocks in nature.

If you return to the same sit spot regularly, over days and weeks and seasons, you will become part of the natural neighbourhood. You'll notice the yellowing of the foliage and the birds that disappear as the temperature drops. You'll notice how the sunlight changes from the cool, crisp blue of the cold months to the harsh, white sunlight of mid-summer. You might learn where the nests are, which seeds the king parrots love to eat, the time of year you can expect to see the common bluebottle butterflies and hear the drone of cicadas.

By slowing down, showing up and paying attention, you become part of a place and it becomes part of you, gradually developing a connection to the rhythm and feel of it—a time-bending homecoming of sorts. As Robin Wall Kimmerer says in her book *Braiding Sweetgrass*, 'Knowing that you love the earth changes you, activates you to defend and protect and celebrate. But when you

connect to the rhythm
and feel of nature

feel that the earth loves you in return, that feeling transforms the relationship from a one-way street into a sacred bond.'

I have two current sit spots, both of which are in my yard. One is among the rose bushes and herbs next to my driveway and the other is lying on the grass in my backyard, looking up through the branches of the chestnut trees in our garden. Neither offers a pristine natural outlook—I can see the house easily from each of them. But I've discovered that it doesn't really matter.

From the little blue bench set among my roses, I look at the plants and soil and sky. I watch the grasshoppers eating my dahlias in summer and the leaves of the Japanese maple and plum trees turn red and purple in autumn. I watch how the lavender and sage and rosemary hold on through the worst of the winter, when the birds mostly move on and the frost can stay thick on the ground until after I've finished my second coffee. I look out for black cockatoos flying overhead, offering their mournful cry that never fails to stir my heart. I am overjoyed when I spot the elusive native blue-banded bee dipping in and out of the spikes of purple lemon balm flowers.

These places are not flashy or impressive but spending time there, simply observing and allowing myself to feel a sense of belonging and connection to this tiny corner of the world, brings me so much contentment. What's more, as I come to see myself as an integral part of this place, I've developed a sense of responsibility for all that happens in it. I make sure I leave plenty of flowers for the pollinators if I'm cutting some to take inside; I leave shallow bowls of water out on hot days, so the skinks, butterflies and bees have something to drink and somewhere to cool off. I relinquish most of my plums to the birds who are often doing it tough by the time mid-summer rolls around. As much as I gain from becoming part of this special place, it's becoming more and more important to me that the soil and plants and birds and insects and animals benefit too.

Get grounded

Have you heard of grounding? Sometimes called 'earthing', it refers to the practice of making contact with Earth's surface by walking barefoot, sitting on the ground or digging in the dirt (there are various devices and gadgets for sale that purport to do the same thing by connecting the user to the ground via electrical current, but considering this book is about making positive changes as accessible as possible, let's focus on the free options). Our modern lifestyles mean that we are indoors and/or wearing shoes the vast majority of the time, effectively reducing our contact with Earth's surface to almost nothing. Scientists now believe that reconnecting with the ground offers us some pretty impressive benefits. While the research is still emerging, one study found that connection with the ground can 'induce multiple physiological changes of clinical significance, including reduced pain, better sleep, a shift from sympathetic to parasympathetic tone in the autonomic nervous system . . . and a blood-thinning effect'. Sounds great, but if we're so far removed from Earth's surface most of the time, what can we do to tap into the benefits of grounding?

Grow something

If you have a backyard, a balcony or even a sunny windowsill inside, why not grow something? You could try herbs, a citrus tree, a pretty pot of geraniums or even throw some seeds in the ground and see what happens. Relish the process of digging over the dirt, scooping up a handful and seeing how it smells and, if you're in the garden, look for worms or other bugs in the soil. By growing something, you become acutely aware of the specific needs of plants and how they will adapt to survive, to a point, but in order to thrive they require the right care—just like us.

Time spent in nature
equals improved
wellbeing for us and
improved wellbeing
of the natural world.
It's a genuine win–win.

While you're digging in the dirt, try walking around your yard or garden barefoot too (unless it's not possible for safety reasons, obviously). Shedding your shoes can also help to strengthen and stretch the muscles, ligaments and tendons in your feet and lower legs; and help to develop core stability and result in less loading on your joints, which in turn can help to prevent osteoarthritis. Plus, it feels nice! Sensing the different textures underfoot, the spiky, smooth, warm and cool surfaces—it's a mindfulness practice.

The bottom line

Imagine for a moment a world where nature is at the centre of everything. All of our homes have windows with views of trees or gardens. All of our neighbourhoods have accessible parklands and walking tracks. Office buildings are all fitted with vertical gardens and have ample sunlight, schools regularly teach classes outside, hospitals are built around central courtyard gardens with every patient able to see, if not directly experience, natural settings every day. A world where taking a weekend off, unplugging, disconnecting from tech and spending time in the wild is normal and where doctors prescribe a weekly dose of forest bathing alongside daily blood-pressure medication and antidepressants.

If we lived with nature in this way, alongside nature, as part of nature, it would be impossible to view ourselves as separate from it, and we couldn't treat her like an afterthought or just a series of resources ready and waiting for us to dig up or cut down, with our eyes firmly on the dollar signs.

The bottom line we should all be interested in when it comes to nature is that time spent in nature equals improved wellbeing for us and improved wellbeing of the natural world. It's a genuine win–win.

Considering we live in a world that is mostly governed by a very different bottom line—the profit/loss, surplus/deficit kind of bottom line—I think we need to offer an equation that appeals to those who work in politics, the policymakers, the gatekeepers, the string-pullers, the fossil-fuel billionaires, the property developers, the bureaucrats stripping funding from our hospitals, our schools, our cultural institutions and giving the green light for more and more of our natural spaces to be demolished for the sake of 'progress'. To these people I offer the following:

- Spending time experiencing nature enhances academic performance in many ways, as shown in a 2019 review of hundreds of studies and published in *Frontiers in Psychology*. Not only does time in nature boost students' performance in reading, writing, maths, science and social studies, but it also enhances their creativity, critical-thinking skills and problem-solving. Even just seeing trees and green spaces from school buildings can foster academic success. Nature-based learning is associated with reduced aggression, greater impulse control and less disruptive behaviour, and spending time in nature can also help children focus their attention and reduce the symptoms of ADHD.

- Employees who are able to spend more time outside, or who work in offices with a view of trees or parkland, report higher levels of happiness, job satisfaction and overall wellbeing, while exposure to the greenery of indoor plants can increase productivity by more than 15 per cent, as found in a 2014 University of Exeter study. Nature—even in small doses—also helps employees to be more creative in their work, which can positively impact their ability to innovate and solve problems. Happier and more satisfied staff equals less turnover, while healthier staff equals fewer sick days, both of which are good for profits.

- Thousands of studies point to the beneficial health outcomes for patients exposed to nature, stretching back to Roger Ulrich's 1984 study that showed a natural view from a hospital window had a positive impact on those recovering from surgery. It's also been discovered that patients who have access to green spaces, or even those whose room features a large photograph of a bright, green wilderness, show improved health outcomes throughout their hospital stay, with convalescence times reduced by more than a day. Not only do they recover more rapidly, but those patients who have some access to viewing or visiting a natural green space also have a reduction in pain and stress levels, which in turn helps to boost their immune system allowing their treatments to work more effectively. Of course, the health implications aren't only physical either, as it's well documented that time spent walking in nature, listening to natural sounds or even viewing natural scenes can help reduce rumination and negative thought patterns, alleviate symptoms of anxiety and increase feelings of calm, clarity and contentment, as discovered by Gregory Bratman of Stanford University in a 2015 study.

There are myriad reasons why we can't or won't increase access to nature (the most common of which seems to be financial), but by shifting to a well-rounded, holistic view, one with the health and wellbeing of individuals and communities at its centre, I think the question really isn't 'Can we afford to do this?' but rather 'Can we afford not to?'

If you feel like you have a voice in one of the spheres of power and influence, I'd encourage you to talk to your boss or manager, or to drop some of these bottom lines into conversation and see where it leads. Perhaps you might want to talk to your housemates, family, colleagues or friends about the way nature has positively impacted your life.

Let's say, however, that calls for change fall on deaf ears. If these ideas still don't inspire change, we need to question the motives of the people in power. Perhaps their decisions are not, as they'd tell us, being driven by a desire to do right by the people, to deliver the best outcomes or services possible, to see students or patients leave their institutions better than when they arrived. Perhaps their motives are more self-serving than that. In which case, a prescription of generosity-inducing, stress-busting, altruism-fuelling nature might just be the thing they need.

Let's tap our inner rebel on the shoulder (remember them?) and not wait for the gatekeepers and policymakers. You have the power to make changes—right now. In your share house or your home, in your workplace or classroom, in your studio or cubicle. Take one of the suggestions from this chapter and apply it without waiting for permission. Bring an indoor plant to your desk. Hang a picture of a wild place in the kitchen. Schedule your next meeting in the park. Take your kids outside to eat dinner once a week. Meet your mates at a park instead of the pub. We are the ones we've been waiting for—and change? It starts with us.

IF YOU HAVE HALF A MINUTE

- Get an indoor plant or two, or put one on your desk at work.

- Create a gallery of photos from your own adventures and keep them on your phone to look at during the day.

- Paint a wall green, change your computer background to an image of a green space, or hang a photo near your workspace of a favourite green scene.

- Try to sit near a window with a green or natural outlook.

- Look for evidence of nature in unlikely places—a nest on a rooftop, plants growing in the cracks of a footpath, wildflowers growing next to the highway.

- When you get home from work, sit on your front step or in your backyard for a few minutes and pay attention to the birds, trees and plants that are part of your natural neighbourhood.

- Stop and smell the roses (literally).

IF YOU HAVE HALF AN HOUR

- Walk around the block in your lunchbreak, looking for trees or counting birds.

- Go to the closest park, take off your shoes and feel the grass beneath your feet.

- Sit under a tree and read a book.

- Write your report by hand, sitting outside, then go back to the office to type it out.
- Take your next meeting outdoors or perhaps make it a walking meeting.
- Walk your dog—choose a new trail or one with more trees or green space.
- Get up ten minutes earlier and drink your tea outside, listening for birds or insects or the breeze in the trees.
- Eat a meal outdoors.
- Cook dinner on your balcony.
- Research if there are any gardens, parks or walking tracks near your office and take time once a week to explore one of them.
- Sit and watch the sunrise or sunset.
- Grow something in a pot or the ground.
- Lie on the grass and look for a four-leaf clover.
- Walk barefoot around your yard.
- Play in fallen autumn leaves.
- Have a snowball fight.

IF YOU HAVE HALF A DAY OR MORE

▼

- Take a group of friends or family camping.
- Go cross-country skiing.
- Rent a paddleboard and spend a day on the lake or river.
- Pack a picnic and head to the beach.

- Jump on a train and explore a (new to you) national park.

- Spend a few hours in your local park, sitting on the grass, walking barefoot, playing frisbee or climbing trees.

- Hike a mountain.

- Find a new bushwalking track.

- Go mountain biking.

- Find the nearest lake and go fishing.

- Find the most remote beach you can and spend some time there, just you and the waves.

- Find a wild place with no wi-fi or phone reception.

- Learn about local plants and spend a few hours foraging for them.

- Find somewhere you'll be completely surrounded by trees—a national park, a reserve, local park—and spend a few hours there, reading or walking or just hanging out.

- Lie outside at night and look for shooting stars or try to count the stars in the sky.

- Have a siesta on the grass in your backyard or a park.

- Find a swimming hole or lake and take a dip.

- Go for a picnic, swing on the swings, play on the grass, lie down and look at the sky through the leaves.

- Next time it's raining, go for a walk, jump in puddles, listen to the sound of the raindrops hitting the leaves overhead, breathe in the smell.

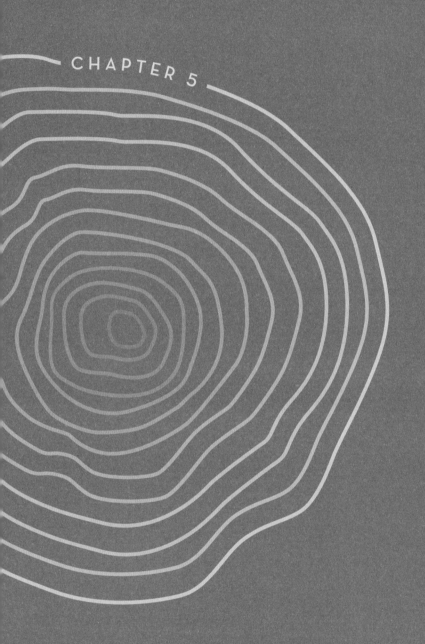

CHAPTER 5

making

My hands

They mix.

They chop.

They stir and they whisk

peaks, soft and glossy

Temporary mountains.

They dig and they bury and coax and feed and water

seeds in the dirt

until a garden emerges

snail-chewed and fragrant.

They knot and they weave and pull and thread

adding knots to a whole

that is more than the sum of its parts

Lumpy ugly blankets

for smooth-cheeked babies.

My hands make

Fire

Tea

Sandcastles

Rainbows in the dirt

The shape of my son's lips on the page

Silly, adolescent poems

About

Making.

It feels as though we have gone full capitalist on creativity.

We tend to only value it if it makes us money, or if it makes our employer money. Musicians are lauded when they sell out bigger and bigger venues. Creative directors are admired and promoted if their advertising campaign results in record sales. An artist becomes a household name once their work reaches a certain pricepoint. We don't attach the same value to the busker who makes enough money to buy a couple of days' worth of groceries, or the employee who takes a risk and fails, and we typically ignore the homespun efforts of the enthusiastic crafter unless they're particularly good, in which case we tell them earnestly, 'You should sell these at markets!'

I've fallen into this trap before, when a resin-jewellery-making hobby accidentally became a full-time job because I needed to justify the time I spent working on it, and the only way to do so was to try to make money from it. Within months of starting my hobby, I'd begun my own little label. The first few local markets were enjoyable (particularly the part where strangers would give me money) but over time I realised that while there were parts of the process I still enjoyed, namely the tinkering and experimentation, they'd been overshadowed by the scale of the work. Yes, I still spent hours creating, but now I needed to create en masse, on deadline, making thirty rings where I used to make one. As I began exhibiting at larger, fancier markets, I was asked about wholesale prices and whether I had local stockists and, if not, would I offer them exclusive distribution. Soon came the commercial gift fairs and the realisation that the prices I was charging would never allow me to be financially sustainable, so then came the business coaching. Within a few years I'd gone from a purely enjoyable creative hobby to grinding through the daily running of a business I never meant to start. From the joy of making to work in no time flat.

We've attached a dollar sign to creativity and so have stripped away what the crafters and gardeners and tinkerers and edge-of-the-notebook doodlers among us know: creating stuff is fun. It's joyful and satisfying and challenging, regardless of whether what we make is permanent (a handknit scarf), temporary (a meal cooked for friends) or even less tangible than that (a dance performed to an audience of one—you, waiting for your porridge to cook). When we make something, we rearrange the very atoms of the world we live in. We shift the order of them around, and, no matter what else comes after, they will never be the same again.

Creativity is inextricably tied to the notion of care and is something that should feel available to us all, but like so many other worthy, powerful ideas, it has been co-opted and overcomplicated, twisted into something that is only valued in monetary terms. It's precisely because of this that I wanted to spend time digging into the joys and hidden power of simply *making* things.

What kind of things can we coax into existence—using our hands, brains, bodies, mouths and actions?

We can make bread or music. We can make paintings. Dance. Pasta. Trinkets and books and letters and sketches on the back of napkins. We make gardens and wonky ceramic bowls and pesto. We bring ideas to life. We make things to wear. Things to eat. Things to look at, to play with, to make ourselves heard. Things to use and things that are useless. Humans are wired to create. We're wired to tell stories and make music and prepare food and build shelter and produce art. We're wired to adorn our bodies and our homes with creations. To offer them as gifts, to treasure them.

None of these things are accidents. Even in the most freakish of circumstances, where the clay soil becomes the perfect consistency for making earthenware pottery, even then, it would never actually form the shape of a bowl without someone shaping it. Never accidentally sit in the sun for the required hours. Never find its way to a pot of glaze. Never fall into a fire and fall back out again once it was ready for use.

Many of us ignore our innate need to make things. We have grown up in a world where convenience is king and the golden glow of the new, the store-bought, the shiny and on-trend is queen. Why bother making something from scratch when we can just order it online and have it delivered to our front door the next day? Within the hour even?

We spend so much of our time in passive consumption mode, inhaling products and food and information, much of it dressed as entertainment or convenience: TV shows, endless news cycles, social media, ready-made meals, fast fashion served up in micro-seasonal trends that are too cheap to ignore.

But when Covid hit, it was like an unconscious collective light bulb went off and suddenly many of us realised that on some deep level we *needed* to make. Perhaps it was because so much of the news was scary, or because so many of yesterday's certainties were now uncertain, that making offered us a distraction. Maybe for some of us it was simply boredom or the very real possibility that our financial situation could soon look quite different and we were going to need to learn how to DIY some of the things we used to buy. Whatever brought it about, many of us found we simply had to use our hands, our brains, our bodies to bring new things into the world.

For a lot of people, that new thing was bread. Perhaps it was the sense of comfort, homeliness, security or nourishment it offered, perhaps it was the smell, or the Instagram bragging rights afforded to anyone who managed to bake a nice-looking loaf of sourdough from scratch.

For others, crafts became the expression of creativity we needed. I finally took the opportunity to start (and surprisingly finish) a baby blanket for my youngest nephew—and was delighted to see that he had outgrown it by the time he received it on his first birthday.

Seedlings and seeds were a hot commodity all of a sudden as thousands of people decided to make a garden. Add to that our very real concerns about food security and there were gardens of all shapes and sizes popping up on balconies, in courtyards and in backyards all over the place.

Some people played music for the first time in years or took the opportunity to learn a new instrument. Some recipe-related searches were up by more than 800 per cent as more people began cooking at home, and the creation of funny videos on TikTok and Instagram skyrocketed.

Whether forcefully or otherwise, our lives slowed down, and for many people that meant we were still enough to hear the inner voice, yearning to make a mark, to leave something behind in an intentional act of creation, an exercise in presence and the joy of bringing something new into being while blocking out the noise of a world that won't stop pushing us to consume, to take, to use up.

Lockdown gave us an opportunity to quieten at least some of that noise, and our collective inner wisdom took the opportunity to whisper quietly in our ears, that maybe that compulsion to constantly *do*, scroll and buy could be better satisfied by the single-mindedness of making.

When we're talking care, both of ourselves and of others, therapy is an incredibly valuable tool, one that I've used many times over the years. But when we talk about therapy, what do we actually mean? Is it solely the domain of psychologists and counsellors, or is there scope for a broader definition of what therapy can look like?

How often have you heard someone refer to cooking or singing or knitting or dancing as their 'therapy'? The suggestion being that it offers them a similar reprieve from the worries and problems of their lives in the same way traditional therapy does. I know I've referred to gardening that way many times over the years, as it allows me to escape again and again: to get outside, to decompress, to distract myself from the stresses and anxieties of day-to-day life. In fact, after I was diagnosed with severe postnatal depression in 2011, I rediscovered myself through the act of making a garden. It was a place where the rush and noise and pressure of life felt distant, where I was able to drift away from much of the deep depression I felt by digging and trimming and mulching and watering and fertilising and planting. All of these fairly simple tasks, all quite repetitive, were so powerful in giving me the space I so badly needed: the ability to get out of my head and away from the noise for an hour or two.

Perhaps you might replace gardening with cooking, knitting, woodworking, whittling, leatherwork, jewellery making, pottery, dancing, singing, writing poetry, sketching, sculpting, painting, playing an instrument, redecorating your living room, arranging your bookshelf by colour, painting your nails or making your own beauty products, or perhaps you've yet to find your therapy. Regardless, it turns out that calling our creative pursuits therapy isn't just a neat way to sum up the personal benefits we experience when making something. In fact, there's a whole heap of research that shows making things is incredibly good for us, so much so that, much like forest bathing, crafting is now being prescribed by GPs and therapists in some parts of the world as an accompaniment to antidepressants. This is known as 'social prescribing', where doctors refer patients to non-clinical therapies such as art and craft classes. The Royal Australian College of General Practitioners has also recommended these kinds of creative prescriptions be incorporated into Australia's healthcare system.

Research has also shown that making things can:

- reduce stress
- activate our parasympathetic nervous system and help us to feel calmer
- help our brain's reward centre release dopamine, the feel-good neurotransmitter
- foster feelings of pride and satisfaction as we learn and master new skills
- elevate our mood
- significantly delay the onset of cognitive conditions such as dementia and Alzheimer's disease
- decrease anxious rumination in people living with various mental illnesses
- improve self-esteem
- increase levels of self-efficacy, which means we're better equipped to face our own challenges and deal with disappointments.

Go with the flow

Making also helps us to meditate, in one form or another. Many acts of making, particularly those that involve repetitive movements such as stirring, stitching and strumming, help our brains to enter a meditative state and in this kind of active meditation we experience many of the same benefits as we would when doing a sitting meditation (think improved sleep, improved memory function and increased self-awareness).

Many acts of making,
particularly those that
involve repetitive
movements such as
stirring, stitching
and strumming, help
our brains to enter
a meditative state.

Related to this idea of active meditation is something called our 'flow state'. Have you ever been so absorbed in making or doing something that you lose track of time? Or that your body seemingly ceases to exist for a moment? That blissful state of engrossment is called a flow state, and much of the research around the role of creativity in happiness and mental wellbeing revolves around the idea of accessing it.

In short, a flow state is powerful: you are simultaneously productive and *feel* great. You don't have to force yourself to work hard; instead, completing the task seems to come almost automatically, as if you are 'flowing' through your work. When we enter a flow state we benefit from a high level of concentration and a feeling of clarity about what needs to be done. We also sense a lack of obstacles as the thoughts and feelings that generally cloud our minds—stress, worry and self-doubt—disappear for a while, at the same time as you find a deep pleasure in whatever you're doing. Mihaly Csikszentmihalyi is the psychologist who first recognised and named the psychological concept of flow and described it as 'the secret to happiness' not only because of the enjoyment of the task at hand but also the general sense of wellbeing, happiness and fulfilment that follow even after you've moved on to do something else.

Csikszentmihalyi's theory is that when we're engrossed in a task that has us operating in a state of flow—knitting a jumper for example—our brains are temporarily unable to process other, non-essential information, which means our physical awareness disappears, pain and discomfort can fade, concerns and stresses and doubts cease to take up real estate in our brains. It leaves us feeling removed from time, removed from our normal reality and all that it entails, giving us a reprieve from discomforts and pains and worries that may otherwise plague us. In short, making heals, and perhaps there's no better story to exemplify this than that of the St Paul's Cathedral altar frontal and the World War I soldiers who made it.

During World War I, millions of soldiers were injured in battle and required long periods of rehabilitation in one of the many hospitals and convalescent homes throughout the world. Many of these soldiers suffered severe injuries including the loss of limbs, spinal injuries and permanent severe pain due to nerve damage or shrapnel wounds, not to mention the tens of thousands who suffered what was then known as 'shell shock' (what we now call post-traumatic stress disorder).

In an attempt to help these soldiers recuperate, and in some instances help them retrain their brains and hands to function again, many were taught handicrafts in convalescent homes in the United Kingdom. Some soldiers learnt basket weaving or leatherwork, while others learnt to embroider. Between the summers of 1918 and 1919, more than a hundred allied soldiers in hospitals and convalescent homes all over England worked on small individual embroidery projects, which were then sent to the Royal School of Needlework in London and stitched onto an altar frontal.

Even though I've only ever looked at it in photos online, I can see that this cloth is genuinely beautiful. I have to admit I was taken aback at how delicately and skilfully it was made, how the intricately stitched birds and flowers and vines are so finely sewn as to look like a watercolour painting rather than needlework. The individual pieces in different shades of blue, green, yellow, purple and gold were created by individual men each locked in their own struggles, who found solace or pride or healing or purpose in their work.

Used for the first time at the national service of thanksgiving for peace at the end of the war in July 1919, the cloth remained in use for many years, until the cathedral was bombed during the London Blitz in World War II. It was long thought that the cloth had been destroyed but it had actually been packed away, survived the Blitz and remained in storage for 70 years, largely forgotten. It was rediscovered by a researcher in 2004 and a team of volunteers spent the better part of a decade restoring the work of the soldiers. Ahead of the centennial commemoration of the outbreak of World War II, researchers at St Paul's tracked down relatives of many of the men who worked on the cloth and invited them to attend a service in August 2014, where the restored altar frontal would be used for the first time in more than seven decades.

Since then the cloth has been used during services commemorating the 100-year anniversary of armistice, and services where hundreds of schoolchildren sang in front of it after studying the lives of the men who created it.

This beautiful piece not only offered therapy and healing to the men who helped make it but also continued to bring people together many years after the last of them was gone. The cloth shows how making can bring healing—both physical and mental—and that making has the capacity to bring us together.

At the heart of this small story lies the question of what might happen if we let the solace and healing and connections of creativity seep into our world? Improved health, peace of mind, an ability to distance ourselves temporarily from pain and suffering: what if we let these ripples spread out, making more ripples and waves as they go? What might that world look like?

Stitch it up

Aside from the very real benefits of living in a society that has significantly improved mental health and higher levels of happiness, contentment and satisfaction, I've also experienced how crafting can

making can bring healing

build community too—this time through a much humbler cloth.
I'm talking about the dishcloth.

I learnt to crochet with a crappy plastic hook and some waxy
cotton twine I bought at an op shop for the princely sum of 50 cents.
Every night, for several weeks, I'd pick up that twine and my plastic
hook and watch YouTube videos on how to create a foundation
chain, how to crochet a single stitch, then a double and then a treble.
I would studiously make a few rows of whatever stitch I was learning
that night, amazed that what felt like an exercise in tying a series
of random knots could add up to something that looked remotely
uniform. Then I would pull it all apart before going to bed. At first,
I wasn't making anything, and it wasn't particularly relaxing either
(learning new things rarely is) but over time I found myself enjoying
it. I made a few wonky scarves and capes for my kids' toys, but it
wasn't until I came across a pattern for the humble dishcloth that
I tried making anything of use.

Long and knotty story short, I managed to make my first dishcloth
(which is basically just a square of crochet), and when I tied off the
yarn and wove the end in, I was ludicrously excited and ridiculously
satisfied. I had made something useful! This dishcloth, this humble
thing that I used to buy from the supermarket by the packet,
something I would use until it was holey and falling apart, that I
would toss into the compost without a second thought, became a
point of significant pride in my life, and the ripples travelled way,
way further than I ever expected.

The first ripples made sense. They were small and personal. I was
genuinely pleased with myself for learning a new skill and sticking
with a project. I eventually found the process of crocheting relaxing
and looked forward to my nightly ritual of stitching a few rows while
I wound down from the day. My sleep improved and I felt motivated
to keep making, keep learning, keep growing.

The ripples then began to reach further as my kids watched me work and asked me to teach them how to crochet. They asked if I could make them something. They began to see making things as a regular part of my life. I then mentioned my dishcloths to family, telling them how I could wash and re-use the same cloths for months before retiring them to the cleaning pile and eventually throwing them in the compost bin. I started to get requests to make cloths for them, so I happily got busy making more.

The ripples reached further still as I developed a greater respect for the skills and energy that go into anything handmade—even the simplest things. I became more determined to look after the things I owned, to mend them, to repurpose them, to dispose of them well once they had no other use. Further still, the ripples continue to move outward as I experiment with ways to reduce consumption even more, to reduce waste, to reduce the pollution created by me, or on my behalf, as I rethink all the things I purchase. This leads me to a place of more resilience, more community-minded solutions, more respect for the skills and knowledge of previous generations. It brings me back to a place of care. For myself, sure, but also for the planet. Making once again reminds me of how connected we are, and how one seemingly insignificant choice can reverberate through homes, communities and workplaces.

Look, I get that it sounds like a lot to come from a dishcloth. And it is. But imagine if each of us had our own version of those ripples, and they reached out from our own version of a dishcloth: making bread, throwing pottery, knitting a blanket, repairing a chair. Imagine how differently we might view the food we eat, the clothes we own, the home we live in, the furniture we fill it with—the conversations and respect and reduction in unnecessary consumption and the pollution that goes along with it—all from caring enough to take the time to make something.

Make it small

In saying all of that though, for an idea that is so inherently positive, making invites a lot of negative self-talk. We throw up a lot of barriers to creativity before we even allow ourselves to begin:

- I'm not creative. (I can't dance/draw/play an instrument/cook/sculpt /sew/knit/paint walls or portraits or nails/do intricate make-up/style hair/build model planes and so on).
- I don't have the time.
- I don't have the money.
- I don't have the space.
- I don't have the skill.
- I don't have access to classes.
- I don't have inspiration.
- I don't know how to start.

I can almost guarantee that even the most prolific creators have thought most of these at some point in their lives. What's more, they may have even been true for a time, just like they may be at different times in your life.

If you've just had a baby, you probably don't have a lot of opportunity to start a new hobby, particularly one with a steep learning curve or one that requires lots of time. If you're living in a share house or with your folks, you might not have any space beyond your bedroom in which to get creative, so large-scale oil painting might not work for you right now. If you've never been exposed to more traditional types of creativity—drawing, painting, textile or fibre art—you may feel intimidated by your lack of the basics. That's okay. It's all okay. Meet yourself where you are: curious about making things.

Ask yourself what you were doing last time you felt that blissed-out sensation of being in a flow state. Were you using your hands? Were you dancing, cooking, daydreaming, writing, gardening or moving furniture around your bedroom? Spending some time asking yourself this might offer insight into the kinds of things you enjoy doing and the sorts of making activities you might want to explore.

Then, remember what we agreed upon in the beginning of the book: get comfortable in the not-knowing. Pick up that magnifying glass again and remember that things don't need to be good or big or impressive in order to make a difference. The benefits we've covered in this chapter all apply regardless of whether you're making the most mundane of items (dishcloths, anyone?) or crocheting a full loungeroom suite for your cat. While there is a particular boost of pride that comes when we finish a project, flow state tells us that intrinsic motivation (i.e. that the thing you're doing is so pleasurable you'd choose to do it no matter the outcome) is one of the most important elements of experiencing flow.

So, look at the kind of making you want to do and then shrink the scale of it. Keep your expectations realistic, keep your scope manageable (I'd even urge you to keep it really, really small on purpose, ego be damned) and see how you feel after playing in that sandbox for five or ten minutes every day.

See what works, see what doesn't. See where the line is between the frustration of learning something new and the frustration of doing an activity that you ultimately just don't enjoy that much.

If money or access to materials or teachings is where you're getting caught, look around at the resources you already have and see if there's something that interests you. Do you have a tin of pencils left over from your school days? Is there a box of odds and ends in your cupboard that you can use to create a birthday card for someone? Do you have an old notepad you no longer use that can be your poetry book? Perhaps a relative or friend knows how to knit and is happy to teach you the basics and loan you some needles in exchange for a homemade meal. Your local community centre might offer craft courses, or you could pick up some introductory guidebooks from your local library. Op shops are great places for finding inexpensive craft materials, and if you don't care about your first projects being particularly fashion-forward you can also pick up patterns, fabric and yarn for next to nothing. Finally, the internet can be a font of inspiration and know-how. I've learnt to grow vegetables, do a decent winged eyeliner, blow-dry my hair and paint a wall from watching people on YouTube. Explore what's available, see who explains things in a way that works for you, then watch their videos and experiment with their techniques.

There is undoubtedly something creative for you to experiment with. So why not try?

IF YOU HAVE HALF A MINUTE

- Wear a new outfit combination.
- Pull out some accessories you haven't worn in a while and play around with them.
- Style your hair differently.
- Listen to music and freestyle dance in your kitchen while you wait for your dinner to reheat.
- Doodle on the train.
- Write one line in your journal every morning.
- Sing a completely made-up song.
- Take a photo a day of something you find beautiful.
- Keep an ideas notebook and add something—a quote, a picture, a leaf, a story—to it every day.
- Make up a story about people you see on the street.

IF YOU HAVE HALF AN HOUR

- Learn how to braid hair.
- Sketch something you can see out the window.
- Choose a problem and daydream outlandish solutions.
- Create a visual journal of your day.
- Write a poem.
- Paint your nails, or someone else's.

PASTE

PASTE

PASTE

PASTE

PASTE

PASTE

PASTE

PASTE

PASTE

PASTE

PASTE

PASTE

PASTE

PASTE

PASTE

- Make a sculpture out of twigs and leaves while you sit in the park.
- Learn to hula hoop.
- Make a batch of playdough and create shapes or words or characters.
- Play with toys—dolls and blocks and miniatures.
- Make something out of LEGO.
- Create a list of writing prompts and respond to one every day.
- Do some colouring in.
- Learn to juggle.
- Make something with paper—aeroplane, origami, birthday card.
- Cook a new meal.
- Bake a cake.
- Challenge yourself to write a 50-word story.
- Practise cursive.
- Journal your dreams.
- Create a new yoga flow.
- Write a letter.
- Learn how to play a new song on an instrument.
- Draw temporary tattoos with henna or a texta.
- Draw in the mud.
- Build a sandcastle.
- Draw with chalk on the footpath.
- Start mending those jeans with the hole in the butt or sew that missing button back on.
- Draw a self-portrait with your eyes closed.

IF YOU HAVE HALF A DAY OR MORE

- Rearrange your bedroom.
- Paint your living room a new colour.
- Create a garden bed and plant it out with seeds you've never grown before.
- Sew something.
- Crochet something (a dishcloth!).
- Write a short story.
- Build a treehouse.
- Make a short video about one of your favourite days/trips/people.
- Create a family dance routine.
- Design a mandala from things you find in your garden.

movement

Long-limbed grasses dance in the wind
like waves rolling in to shore
as my feet connect
to the cool damp earth.

Together we walk ancient trails,
breathe ancient smells.
Together we feel our skin warm
as our blood, like a spring-swollen river
flows impatiently.

Our shoulders shake
as we pull our bodies up and over
squatting on a red rock
while our fingers tingle with scrapes hard-won.
When hips and knees and elbows bend,
pulling muscles, pushing bone,
taking us to sights never seen and
sensations as familiar as
our own breath filling our ears.

We return, mud-caked and light,
limbs beautiful and trembling,
hearts brimming with knowing
and feet exultant,
already craving the cool damp earth again.

Want to know how to make a minute feel ten times longer?

Try holding the plank position for a full 60 seconds and see how time drags (seriously—how long can one minute take?) Or practise tree pose for thirty seconds and feel the slow crawl of each and every one of them as your leg quivers and you try to stay upright.

Now, before I go any further, I just want to tell you that this chapter is not about exercise. It's not clad permanently in activewear, it doesn't have a VIP gym membership and it won't post any #fitspo content to your feed. Instead, it's about movement. For some, it might be a simple case of semantics, where 'exercise' and 'movement' are different words used to describe the same thing. To me, there is a big difference between the two because, while exercise brings many benefits, it also carries expectations, ideals and comparisons, a certain kind of competitiveness and the possibility of failing. In fact, the years I was a consistent activewear-clad gym-goer were punctuated by feelings of failure rather than achievement. I didn't exercise because of the joy it brought me; I went to the gym because I thought I should. I went because I had in mind a particular gold standard and thought I needed to work until I reached it. So, if I didn't lose weight, if I didn't go down a jeans size, if I didn't have a flat stomach, if I didn't get glowing skin, if I didn't beat my PB, if my arms were never as sculpted as Michelle Obama's, I felt like my efforts had failed.

I mean, we've all seen the 'before and afters', the 'You Won't Believe What She Looks Like Now!' articles, the taut tummies and peachy booties of Instagram, and on some level absorbed the idea that our bodies need to be different—*better*—before they're 'beach-ready' or desirable or healthy or acceptable. (Just a friendly heads-up: they don't.)

Movement, by comparison, feels simple. If you wiggle your fingers, open and close your mouth, shrug your shoulders, straighten your spine, walk to the office printer, stretch before getting out of bed, squat down to play with your dog, repeatedly bend and straighten as you hang clothes on the line—that's movement. To me movement feels less results-oriented than exercise and, with its only goal being movement itself, we succeed simply by moving. What follows from here is a celebration of the simplicity, the accessibility, the joy, the warmth, the benefits and yes, the care that come with moving.

Like many of the types of care we've already looked at, movement has lots of personal benefits that qualify it as self-care, including:

- improved mood
- decreased feelings of stress, anxiety and depression
- increased production of endorphins, leading to more positive feelings and reduced perception of pain
- increased energy levels
- improved insulin sensitivity
- improved cardiovascular fitness
- decreased blood pressure
- increased production of antioxidants
- improved brain function
- increased size of the brain's hippocampus, which helps long-term memory storage
- improved cognitive function
- reduced risk of developing Alzheimer's disease
- increased relaxation

- improved sleep quality
- **reduction in chronic pain**
- improved sex drive
- **increased levels of HDL (good cholesterol)**
- decreased levels of unhealthy triglycerides.

What's so often missing from the conversation about increasing movement, though, are the wider, social benefits. For example, we know that movement boosts production of endorphins in our brain, which makes us feel happier. In turn, feeling happier can lead us to have more positive conversations, to make more connections and to build new friendships or deepen our existing ones, which leads to stronger bonds within our circle of friends, family and the wider community. We also know that simply by walking outdoors regularly, we not only reduce stress levels and improve our cardiovascular health but also have the opportunity to connect with the people we see (particularly if we choose to unplug), the places we walk through and the comings and goings of our neighbourhood. This can foster feelings of familiarity and a sense of belonging to a place, which can lead to higher levels of involvement in community programs and a reduction in loneliness. In addition, we know movement improves our overall mental and physical health, which reduces pressure on the healthcare system and, over time, leads to a reduction in public-health spending for many chronic diseases— money that can instead be spent on education, conservation, renewable energy projects or revitalisation of urban green spaces. I could keep going but I think you can see how powerful and far-reaching the effects of movement can be.

sit less, move more

Sit less, move more

The human body is not suited to sitting for extended periods. Our skeletal structure means we're better adapted to extended periods of walking, squatting, standing and lying down. In fact, humans only began sitting on chairs regularly a little over 200 years ago, when the industrial revolution made the mass production of furniture possible; before that, sitting in chairs was something you did at church or if you were nobility. It was even more recently—in the early-1900s, when conveyor belts were installed in factories and employees had to sit while working, and in the 1940s, when the office as we know it came into being—that sitting became a significant part of the working day for many people. Since then, as convenience and transport options and screen-based work has increased across much of the world, our time spent sitting has skyrocketed. Add to that the fact that many of our downtime activities involve being sedentary too—watching TV, playing video games, online shopping, reading, chatting with friends over a coffee, watching movies— and it's not particularly surprising to learn that, according to the Australian Heart Foundation, the average Australian adult spends more than nine hours per day sitting (far longer than we tend to sleep, which averages around seven hours a night).

In 2018 the Australian Government released updated health advice, designed to help combat the status quo of sedentary behaviour. What was revolutionary about this advice was that, contrary to previous campaigns, it wasn't encouraging people to increase their level of exercise or to make significant dietary changes. The suggestion instead was that we would all benefit from one simple change: 'Sit less, move more.' While it's a problematic recommendation for the wheelchair users among us, this advice did represent a change of direction for public health guidelines, one that seemed to take into consideration our busy lifestyles and increased sedentary behaviour. It also appeared to acknowledge the many studies that show the best way to combat sedentary behaviour is to build more habitual movement (not necessarily exercise) into our days, in the same way we turn drinking enough water and brushing our teeth into everyday habits. (Many of these studies have found that while exercise offers many benefits, an hour of exercise every couple of days is not enough to undo the damage done if the remainder of our time is sedentary.

Okay, but what about the real reason we don't move more? The one that says we don't have time. Here's where we get to reframe both the idea of moving more, and the idea of not having enough time.

Deskercise

For those days when you're stuck at your desk and are unable to get outside to take even a brief break, there's always deskercise (aka: exercise at your desk). While this might seem like the ultimate in modern-day multi-tasking ridiculousness, these super simple suggestions can be surprisingly helpful in maintaining flexibility, reducing tension and relieving stress—partly due to the brief mental reprieve mini movement breaks afford, and partly due to the health benefits of even the simplest of stretches.

Hopefully it goes without saying that if any of these movements feel painful, please stop. If you've got injuries or are worried about adding new movements into your daily activity, check in with your doctor or a health professional first.

SEATED STRETCHES

- Shrug your shoulders up and down several times, holding the shrug for a second or two at a time.

- Roll your shoulders forward ten times, then roll them backwards ten times—take it nice and slow as you feel the tiny creaks and pops that accompany the action.

- Drop your chin towards your chest and feel the gentle stretch at the back of your neck, then imagine drawing a big circle, clockwise, with the tip of your nose as you slowly rotate your head five times. Repeat anticlockwise.

- Straighten your left arm out in front of your body and turn your palm up to the ceiling, then, using your right hand, gently stretch your fingers down towards the floor, stretching your wrist and forearm. Hold this for ten seconds and then repeat for the right arm.

- Take your left arm across your chest and use it to hug your right shoulder, then use your right arm to deepen the stretch and push your left elbow closer to your chest. Hold for ten seconds and repeat on the right side.

- Straighten both arms above your head, clasp hands together and reach up towards the ceiling, arching your back slightly as you do. Take some deep belly breaths and hold for thirty seconds.

- Keeping your feet on the floor, scoot your backside to the back of your chair and slide your feet forward to extend your legs. Slowly lower your chest towards your knees until you feel a gentle stretch in the back of your legs. Hold for thirty seconds.

- Staying seated, place both feet flat on the floor and turn to look over your right shoulder. Put your right hand on the back of your chair and your left hand on your right knee, and gently twist your body to the right. Take a deep breath in, and as you exhale, try to deepen the stretch a little more, imagining your spine is a wet towel getting wrung out with each breath. Hold for thirty seconds and repeat on the left side.

STANDING STRETCHES

- Stand with both feet flat on the ground and slowly raise yourself up to stand on your tiptoes. Hold for thirty seconds.

- Rest the toes of your left foot against a wall, your desk or your chair and gradually lean forward, stretching out the back of your lower leg. Hold for thirty seconds and repeat on the right side. (If you're wearing rigid-soled or high-heeled shoes, you might want to slip them off for this one.)

- Stand up behind your chair and place your hands on the top of the back rest. Walk your feet back until you can bend forward with your back straight and arms extended. Bend your knees slightly to deepen the stretch in your lower back or straighten them to feel the stretch in your hamstrings. Hold for thirty seconds.

- Stand tall and straight and raise your hands above your head. Rise up to your tiptoes if you can and clasp your hands together as you stretch up towards the ceiling for thirty seconds.

All of these movements can be done at your desk but can also be added to your morning or evening rhythm to increase the amount of movement you do during the day. You can practise several of them while you're cooking dinner, while you wait to pick the kids up from school, in the car, on the train or in the lift. You don't need to wait until you have a specific timeslot set aside for movement, you can simply add these and other small movements to your day and benefit from the many advantages of regular stretching such as finding an increase in flexibility and range of motion, increased blood flow, improved posture, reduction in back pain, stress relief, a decrease in tension headaches, a reduction in fatigue and improved productivity. This kind of simple, seemingly insignificant self-care can have ripple effects all the way through your daily life.

Get incidental and intentional

To untangle the knots of our deeply sedentary lifestyle (and the knots of our deeply tensioned shoulders), we need to learn to think creatively about how to bring more movement into our days. By making simple, if unconventional, changes to the way we structure our days and our downtime—not to mention our kitchens, workplaces and living spaces—we can significantly increase not only the range of movements we do, but also the amount of movement.

Some of these suggestions might feel more achievable than others, but to get you thinking creatively about some of the possibilities in your own life, here are some of the shifts you can make to ensure that your days become more movement-rich.

SIT ON THE FLOOR

Sitting at a low coffee table to eat or work gives you the opportunity to stretch your legs in different ways for longer periods of time, and it also means you need to get back up at some stage, a process that engages a wide variety of movements.

~~~~~

STAND TO WORK

Use a few hefty books or boxes to create a standing desk (check online for some great guidelines on how best to align your workspace for back and neck health) and try working on your feet for part of the day. Combine this with calf stretches and heel raises to add some more movement. You could also try standing on public transport rather than sitting—by gently engaging your core muscles, try to remain stable and steady as the train, bus or tram accelerates and slows down.

~~~~~

REARRANGE YOUR CUPBOARDS

By putting the items you use most frequently in low cupboards, you'll find yourself squatting and bending many times during the day, using big muscles like your thighs and glutes more than you would if your pantry, cutlery and saucepans were at waist height.

~~~~~

MULTI-TASK YOUR MOVEMENT

When doing things such as folding laundry, cooking, reading, cleaning or gardening, incorporate some additional movement. Get down in a wide-legged squat when you're weeding the veggie garden or do some lunges when watering your pot plants. If you're reading or watching TV, try lying on your back and doing some spine twists.

~~~~~

WALK A LITTLE FURTHER

It's an oldie but a goodie—get off the bus one stop early and walk the extra distance home or take the slightly longer route to uni. Find a coffee shop an extra block or two away and walk there for your morning fix, or take some of your phone calls outside, walking

We don't need to make
huge sweeping changes
to our daily rhythms
in order to add more
movement to our lives.

or stretching as you talk. You could also try taking the stairs rather than the lift and parking further away from your destination. By setting a timer for every thirty minutes and taking a two-minute walk around the office or to the bathroom and back, you could potentially add more than half an hour of walking to your day, every day.

The bottom line is we don't need to make huge sweeping changes to our daily rhythms in order to add more movement to our lives. Just look out for the opportunity to incorporate more and see how much of a difference it makes.

Yoga

Yes, yes, I know, it wouldn't be an even remotely woo-woo book without talking about yoga at least once, but the truth is that yoga offers us so many opportunities for care that go far beyond those of simple stretching (even though the benefits to our flexibility, strength and circulation are also worth celebrating).

When we practise yoga, particularly if we do it consistently, we learn how to tap into the mind–body connection. At its simplest, the mind–body connection is the two-way street that runs between your body and your mind. How we feel physically can impact our mental state, while at the same time, how we feel emotionally can have a direct and powerful impact on how our body feels. Just look at how your body responds when you're experiencing stress. You might be worried about finances or relationship troubles, but the mental stress you're experiencing has adverse effects on your physical health. You could feel sick in the stomach, or tense in the neck and shoulders, perhaps you get headaches, or a stomach ulcer, or high blood pressure as a result of experiencing stress. If you travel the other way down the street, physical problems such as back pain or a knee injury can often lead to feelings of depression, anxiety and stress as we grapple with bodily limitations or the mental health impacts of chronic pain.

Yoga is a way to harness this mind–body connection in a positive way and asks us to spend time noticing how they're inextricably linked. Over time, this allows us to develop a much greater level of physical awareness and appreciation for the present moment. Despite what Insta-yoga-land might suggest, this isn't about physical appearance or beautiful handstands, but rather paying attention to what our bodies do and how we feel when they do it.

As I've practised yoga on and off over the years, I've learnt what it feels like to release the muscles in my upper back when I'm hanging loose in a standing forward bend, and I've similarly learnt to recognise the rush of endorphins when it happens. I can't help but smile and sigh with pleasure when my upper spine stretches out towards the floor and I know that, if nothing else, I'll leave the mat with that feeling fresh in my mind and a small spark of gratitude to my body for allowing me to experience it. It's a surprisingly loving— and lovely—feeling.

Lest you feel like you need to spend an hour on the mat in order to feel the benefits, rest assured, many mornings all I have available to me is the few minutes it takes for the kettle to boil, and when I use that time to practise a few mountain poses, some deep breathing and a sun salutation or two, I still feel elevated, looser and more clear-headed. A 2012 study by Dr Alyson Ross, published in *Evidence-Based Complementary and Alternative Medicine,* surveyed more than a thousand yoga practitioners and discovered that it was the *frequency* of practice as opposed to the length of the session that contributed to positive outcomes.

The more frequently someone practised yoga, the higher the likelihood of increased levels of wellbeing, mindfulness, fruit and vegetable consumption, quality sleep and reduced levels of fatigue. So, don't let a lack of time stop you. Even if you can only carve out a few minutes a day, you'll find literally thousands of free, short yoga classes online to help get you started if you don't have the toolkit already.

Meditation in motion

Combining the enormous benefits of meditation (reduced negative emotions, new perspective on stressful situations, increased self-awareness) with the benefits of movement is to get the best of both worlds.

While practising 'meditation in motion' with tai chi or qi gong is a great way to combine movement and mindfulness, you can also turn virtually any mundane physical task into a meditative practice.

Take chopping vegetables, for example. Most of the time, we breeze through without paying any attention to the experience itself, but by choosing to treat the action as meditation in motion, this once-humdrum task can be elevated to something else entirely. Start by feeling the shape and texture of the vegetables—whether they're smooth or rough, soft or hard, heavy or light. Then feel how that changes as you wash them, how they feel in your hands, whether the sound of the running water changes when it runs over different kinds. Then, as you begin to peel or chop, pay close attention to the tiny movements in your hands, arms and shoulders, the way your fingers hold the knife, the feel of it as it hits the chopping board, the snap, slice or squash as you cut through each vegetable. Feel how your body weight shifts slightly from foot to foot with each movement, how you feel if you relax your shoulders slightly. Notice the scents too—when the chilli smells the most pungent, when the earthiness of the potato is at its richest. Simply by paying attention to seemingly insignificant movements or senses, you're tapping into the body–mind connection and learning to be aware of the present moment. (You're also using your Time-bending superpower).

You can practise moving meditations while washing the dishes, mopping the floor, deadheading your roses, painting your front door, rearranging your lounge room, doing the grocery shopping, making the bed, mowing the lawn or any other everyday, so-common-it's-invisible task.

Similarly, you can practise walking meditation too, if you're willing to use your Unplug tool for a few moments. This takes the same basic idea as the above meditation in motion but applies it to a walk (or even just a portion of a walk). Try taking out your earbuds, slow down your walking pace and start by paying attention to your feet as they hit the ground. Feel the rhythm and the way it reverberates up your shins. Do you strike with your heel first, or do you walk more flat-footed? What happens to those sensations if you soften your jaw and let your shoulder blades slide down your back? Then, looking around, what do you see? Look at the colour of the sky, the texture of the footpath, the names of the shops you walk past, the different fonts on the street signs. Take a moment to feel your breath moving in and out of your chest and your arms as they swing by your side. This is an exercise you can adapt to do whether you use a wheelchair or a mobility device, if you're indoors or out. The circumstances matter far less than the intention to simply pay attention.

Become a flâneuse

A flâneuse (or a flâneur in the male form) is defined as 'someone who walks around not doing anything in particular but watching people and society'. A person who strolls, saunters or loafs: someone who enjoys the art of flânerie. In her 1927 essay of the same name, Virginia Woolf rather delightfully refers to it as 'street haunting'.

In an effort to incorporate more movement (not to mention more connection, more time outdoors, more creativity and imagination and idle wandering), why not become someone who practises the art of flânerie and take a stroll through your neighbourhood? Not for exercise or to achieve a certain number of steps, but for the benefit of noticing while moving. Take your flânerie as an invitation to unplug and pay attention to the people, places, trees, flowers, comings and goings in your neighbourhood. Notice the colours and scents, the change of seasons, the new faces, the familiar patterns, the cats and dogs and birds. They all make up the specific corner of the world in which you live, and walking as you observe all of them gives you a chance not only to feel like a part of the collective, but also to engage in an imagining of the lives of those around you. The joys and dramas and cycles of the people, flora and fauna you see on a regular basis. Over time, you may just find that you begin to feel a sense of belonging to the natural rhythms of your neighbourhood, and in doing so, develop a deeper sense of care for it too.

Go barefoot

We've already explored the benefits of 'grounding' in Chapter 4 and how spending time with our bare feet on the earth offers a range of health benefits, but there's also a body of research that suggests going barefoot as much as possible—both indoors and outdoors— is good for us. Wearing shoes changes the way we walk, the way we experience the surfaces we walk on and the way the bones, muscles and tendons in our feet move and react. In a 2019 article in *Medicine & Science in Sports & Exercise*, researchers described how even 'supportive' shoes lead to the development of smaller, weaker muscles in the feet and often result in foot and leg injuries. A solution, they suggested, was to spend more time barefoot in order to develop stronger, more flexible feet that are less prone to injury.

If you want to experiment with going barefoot more, you might need to start out slowly, with a few minutes at a time at home, or in the office if you can get away with it (woolly socks are perfect for cold days), before you progress to short barefoot stints in the garden, at the park or on the beach. It may feel a little odd or uncomfortable at first; rest assured it can take some getting used to, as our long-cosseted feet adjust to the free-range lifestyle.

As you experiment with being barefoot, pay attention to how your feet feel, whether you experience different sensations, or a loosening or tightening of different parts of your feet, ankles and legs. Play around with spreading your toes out wide, rolling from heel to toe and back again, standing tall on your tiptoes and trying to balance your weight evenly across your entire foot.

You also don't need to be barefoot all the time in order to experience the benefits. Even a slow, short, sensation-filled walk across wet grass is an exercise not only in going barefoot, but also in mindfulness and movement.

If, after some experimentation, you're curious about going a little further afield, you could try barefoot bushwalking. The first time I heard about it, I thought it sounded a little dangerous—I mean, walking barefoot in the Australian bush, with her rocky tracks and ants and spiders and snakes, surely, it's an invitation to disaster?

It was an idea I couldn't quite shake though, so one day, I took myself off for a bushwalk along one of my favourite tracks in the Blue Mountains. It winds down from a rocky platform and runs alongside a creek—where the ground is cool and damp on even the hottest summer afternoon, the rock worn smooth by countless years of flowing water. Along the creek banks you can find remnants of

Even a slow, short,
sensation-filled walk
across wet grass is
an exercise not only
in going barefoot, but
also in mindfulness
and movement.

axe-grinding grooves created by the local Dharug people and the track takes you to a cave where layers of ancient Indigenous art— handprints and stencils—are still visible, thought to be somewhere between 500 and 1600 years old.

I walked to the cave in the normal fashion—wearing shoes, moving at a quick pace to get my heart rate up, looking for familiar waypoints so I could track my progress—but I decided to try my return barefoot. I took off my shoes and socks, tied the laces together and slung them around my neck. I flexed my toes on the dusty ground and started walking.

What a revelation.

From the very beginning I was forced to slow down to avoid any sharp rocks or bitey ants. I became aware of every change in temperature underfoot as I travelled from sunshine to shade and back again. I began to notice the subtle and constant difference in the texture of the ground, the way some parts of the track were worn smooth where others were rough and gravelly, how the mud squished between my toes and how some parts of the track felt almost like silk underfoot.

As my feet woke up, so too did the rest of my senses. I could hear more clearly the lyrebird's mimicry and see more clearly the changing colours of the rocks. I could smell the damp soil and eucalypts and, for a time, I felt part of it all. I felt connected. I walked past a huge gum tree, her ghostly bark smooth and pale. I stopped and put my hands on her enormous trunk and was shocked by how cool it felt, as though it were a canvas water-bag full to bursting. I wrapped my arms around her, rested my cheek on her trunk and breathed deeply.

It took me twice as long to do the return trip but by the time I got back to my car, I had a ridiculous grin on my face and a lightness in my heart that I still remember to this day, even though this walk happened years ago. What's more, my feet felt different—more alive and more sensitive—a feeling that lasted for weeks.

I remember starting that walk feeling itchy and cranky, frustrated about something I've completely forgotten now but as I walked back to my car, feet firmly connected to the earth, I realised that so many of my ills—poor temper, headache, irritability—had simply drifted away. That walk and what I felt was an antidote to the stressors of modern life, both physical and mental. Over the years I've found myself craving this same experience and, every time I listen to the quiet voice urging me to take off my shoes and get my feet dirty on the track, I'm reawakened to the all-consuming experience and the heightened senses all over again. I never regret it (although my kids often do . . . 'Come on, Mum, you're taking so long!').

Whether you have time to spare or not, finding small ways to include more movement in your day opens you up to so many more opportunities to get mindful, to feel supported, to connect to your body and to feel what it is to be truly alive. It might seem like simple stretching or a wander around the neighbourhood, but the reverberations from these acts of Small Care shouldn't be underestimated. Connection to mind, body, people, place and planet breeds understanding and empathy, responsibility and ownership. It ties us closer to each other and the places we share.

IF YOU HAVE HALF A MINUTE

- Sit back from your computer and do ten shoulder shrugs or ten neck rolls.
- Stand up and stretch your arms up and over your head.
- Squat to get the pegs while hanging the laundry, feeding the dogs or folding towels.
- Do some calf raises while waiting for your coffee.
- Stretch your wrists and hands while waiting in line at the supermarket.
- Set an alarm for every thirty minutes and, each time it rings, stand up, walk around your office, and then continue working in a new position (standing, sitting at a low table, on a Swiss ball etc.).
- Drink more water so you're forced to take more bathroom breaks and mini-movement breaks during the day.
- Choose a coffee shop further away and walk the extra distance mindfully.
- Jog in place while waiting for documents to print.
- Do thirty star jumps every time there's an ad break on TV.
- Take off your shoes and walk on pebbles or a rough surface.
- Take your phone calls standing up.

IF YOU HAVE HALF AN HOUR

- Rake leaves or shovel snow.
- Start a pick-up game of soccer, cricket or basketball in your backyard or at the park.
- Take an online class: try dance, yoga, tai chi or qi gong.
- Ride your bike to work, school or the shops.
- Walk your kids to school.
- Be a flâneuse.
- Get off the bus one stop early and walk the extra distance.
- Skip rope and practise your old schoolyard moves.
- Have a kitchen dance party.
- Practise cartwheels, handstands or somersaults.
- Climb a tree.
- Weed your garden and alternate between a low squat and kneeling.
- Turn your compost heap by hand.
- Get into house cleaning with an energetic playlist and some elbow grease.
- Chop and grind your ingredients for dinner manually rather than buying pre-chopped ingredients or using the food processor.

IF YOU HAVE HALF A DAY OR MORE

- Go for a slow, barefoot bushwalk.

- Head to the beach or local pool and practise diving or catching waves.

- Host a backyard or park picnic with games (try quoits, pétanque, cornhole, frisbee, Finska and the like).

- Spend a few hours building something for the garden—some tomato trellises, a pea tepee, a climbing frame for pumpkins, watermelons or cucumbers.

- Go bouldering or visit a climbing gym with your kids or some friends.

- Rearrange your kitchen cupboards so that the most commonly used items are down low.

CHAPTER 7

play

Bangagrang!

As he scrapes the scum

from the surface of the pond.

In its forgotten depths

see—

the sweetness of colour,

the cacophony of touch,

the loose tide of time,

gem-sparkled earth and

everywhere

magic.

How we float

how we drift

how we allow ourselves

to swim lazily in the water.

We don't worry about the twisting hands

about the end

about the setting of the sun.

Until we look up and see

the stars on their nightly quest

and we meet them in the molten lilac sky.

I was nervous to write this chapter.

I know that I have been too self-conscious to play in the past, too afraid to do it wrong, too embedded in my adult brain, thinking my very important adult thoughts about very important adult business. Play just wasn't in my DNA, so how could I write about it?

But if play wasn't in my DNA, why would I choose to:

- sit in a modified carriage, propelled around a track at heart-pounding speeds, lifted to great heights and plunged back towards the earth, screaming my lungs out, hands in the air
- spend a blissfully unproductive hour colouring in
- play loud music and twirl around my house with rhythmless abandon
- take a beautiful picture, break it into 1000 odd-shaped pieces and spend a weekend trying to put it together again
- run away from my kids and hide under my bed, stifling the giddy laughter that rises in my throat, trying not to give away my position as they search the house
- slide down a grassy hill on a flattened old moving box, squealing, only to run back to the top of the hill and do it again and again and again
- stand at the top of a snow-covered mountain, click two lengths of fibreglass and wood to my feet and slide on them all the way to the bottom, only stopping to look out at the valley below.

And, given all of these choices, why did I spend so much of my adult life believing that I wasn't a playful person? It turns out the problem wasn't me. The problem was what I thought play had to look like.

For the longest time I believed that play needed to be the obvious kind. The childish, exuberant, quick to laugh, first in line to tell a joke or start a game of charades kind of play. The kind of fully immersive, get on the floor with toys, make-believe play that abandoned me around high school. I didn't realise that visiting an interactive museum exhibition was play, or that carving a watermelon for Halloween (my preferred southern hemisphere option) was play. I didn't realise that making up one-word-at-a-time stories around the dinner table was play or sliding down a waterslide or experimenting with hairstyles or practising crow pose was play. But they are. Play can be as delightfully varied as people are.

In fact, that's part of the problem when it comes to defining just what play is. While its benefits are very real and very powerful, even the psychologists who've built careers studying it find it difficult to accurately describe, because what constitutes play for one person is stressful, boring or frustrating for another. The only widely agreed-upon definition of play is that it's needless, involves some aspect of imagination, leisurely (not to be mistaken with easy), enjoyable and fun, and the motivation to do it is intrinsic, that is, it comes from the process, rather than the outcome. All of which means I'm not going to write a list of reasons why play is good for you and why you should do it because that would take a needless, enjoyable activity and turn it into a should. A need. A to-do. It would be to go full adult on play—and there's no real fun in that, is there?

I suppose though, the question does need to be asked: why do so many adults struggle to be playful?

We adulterate play

As we grow up many of us become more serious versions of our younger selves, stuck in the turning cogs of life, less likely to slip spontaneously into playfulness. In my own, very unscientific research (i.e. conversations I've had with people I know—most of whom are parents), there is a heaviness that seems to attach itself to play once we have kids. On the face of it this seems counter-intuitive. Wouldn't having kids make us more likely to spend time in play mode, not less? In my experience, the answer has been a definitive not-so-much because, while I found myself playing more frequently, rarely did it feel light or loose or enjoyable, like play used to feel when I was young. It often felt (forgive me) like a chore. It felt like something I had to do because, as parents, we know that children learn through play and benefit enormously from it, as do our relationships with them. I was playing with them to help their development and deepen our bonds—things I both wanted and needed to do. By definition, it was not play, for me. When I pair this with my mistaken belief that play was solely the domain of the young, it's little wonder I felt heavy and guilty about it much of the time.

I'm not advocating for a world where we stop worrying about serious issues in order to play LEGO all day. But if play inspires awe and wonder in us, if it promotes creativity and problem-solving, if it encourages empathy and compassion (which it does), how might it improve our efforts in solving serious, grown-up problems and making the world a more compassionate, egalitarian place?

Poverty and inequality and voter suppression and corporate greed and political corruption will not be played away but don't worry that stepping away from these problems in order *to* play means you will miss an opportunity to enact change. Your advantage will be the different perspective you bring when you return. The questions you ask, the assumptions you jettison, the lightness you feel—these can all be agents and catalysts for real change.

Something else I keep returning to in my own exploration of play is that in order to try to recapture some of that lightheartedness I experienced as a kid, I often turned to drinking. Being drunk wiped out my inhibitions, let me dance freely and laugh loudly, head thrown back. It afforded me a heavy-handed kind of playfulness and allowed me to be funny, daring and, honestly, a bit of a pain in the arse sometimes.

I wonder whether the reason (or at least one of the reasons) many people drink or use drugs is to regain that sense of lightness and freedom we used to have as children. When it was okay to dance in the middle of the supermarket, you sang for the joy of it and didn't give a hoot whether it sounded any 'good'. Drinking offers a buffer of confidence or self-assuredness, whereas sober playfulness somehow feels more vulnerable.

We turn play into a competition

As adults, I think we're scared to appear immature in our play, so we avoid all but the sanctioned kind of play—competitive play— or mistake play for simply another kind of work. We believe that if we're going to spend time playing, we need to see measurable, quantifiable benefits. Purposeless, needless, leisurely, intrinsically motivated—these ideas don't really compute in a society fixated on efficiencies. If life is a series of tick-boxes, play doesn't feature on the to-do list.

Fitness-related or competitive play are some of the only types of 'acceptable' play that adults engage in. It's not widely accepted to finger paint or make daisy chains or build sandcastles or play imaginary games (unless, of course, you're doing it with, or for, kids), but strapping on some footy boots and trying to win a game is, because the aims are clear: to get fit, to follow the rules and score more points than the other team.

Even playing a musical instrument is an example of our complicated relationship with play. Learning the ukulele is fine, but it's really

capture the lightheartedness
of a child

only seen as productive if you're practising your chords, learning your songs and making obvious progress. Tooling around, seeing what chords sound good to your untrained ear, feeling how the strings reverberate—that's a waste of time. Where's the recognisable song? Where's the measurable improvement? Where's the output that shows, yes, I am being productive in my downtime?

Work =/= Play

Drawing a distinction between play and work is difficult for a lot of reasons, made more so for those who work for a company that's trying to embrace the 'play at work' philosophy. In an effort to both incentivise employees and create a work environment that maximises productivity, there's been a big push by large organisations to incorporate play into their office space (at least in pre-Covid times). While there is research suggesting that amenities such as a games room or basketball hoop, or department vs department scavenger hunts are good for morale, and a paper by Erin Woolf published in *Management Research Review* in 2014 suggested they also resulted in higher levels of engagement and better creative performance, is at-work 'fun' still fun? I mean, if these things are genuinely enjoyable to employees, then that's a good thing. But when work–life balance is such a challenge for so many people already, maybe this is just another example of wellness trends being turned into shoulds, have-tos, need-tos?

Perhaps the answer isn't to enforce play at work, or believe that all work needs to be enjoyable, but rather to create a system that encourages employees and business-owners and freelancers and work-at-home parents and students to strike a better balance between work and not-work, opening up time for them to find their own types of play away from the workplace. Perhaps even acknowledging that the reason employees may be stressed or getting sick or resigning isn't because they lack play at work, but because they feel pressured to answer emails at night, they no longer feel the weekend is a respite from the office, or insecure work arrangements mean that they always feel on-call.

Waste of time

It might seem like a waste of time to daydream or doodle without any particular purpose—but the truth is we cannot operate at full capacity all the time, and the 'wasted time' that play represents is downtime, which is vital for our wellbeing.

What we're really grappling with when we see play as a time waster is our perception of what's worthwhile.

Yes, there is a good deal of research explaining the importance of play for both children and adults, but I find myself wondering if it's the unquantifiable benefits that are just as, if not more, worthy of our time:

- the elevated feeling after dancing around your living room
- the single-minded peace of learning how to make pottery
- the shared jokes and sense of belonging that stem from the mud-fight you had with friends
- the never-ending renditions of 'Mustang Sally' from your karaoke afternoon
- the sense of shared connection that comes from playing a pick-up game of basketball with strangers.

There is nothing wasted in these experiences. In fact, they fill the gaps between work, family, school, community and all the various obligations we have in life, forming a vital buffer of lightness, fun and meandering joy between the often more pressing requirements of adulthood. Without these buffers, we might find ourselves becoming what we've tried so hard to avoid—inefficient and unproductive.

What would happen if we prioritised play?

Imagine, for a moment, a world where play is encouraged, where it's no longer seen as immature or a waste of time or something we *have* to do with our kids, but rather as a vital part of any day, as important as drinking water or getting enough sleep. Given what psychologists have already discovered about play and its benefits, we would be looking at a world where cooperation and collaboration are the norm, as opposed to individualism and an all-pervasive, me-first mentality. A world where we feel lighter and more energetic, where our mental health and relationships are strengthened and we feel a sense of belonging, trust and connection. Where we spend time simply enjoying activities for no reason other than they're enjoyable, and where devoting an hour to sketching or daydreaming or geo-caching or playing board games is not a waste of time but an important part of our everyday lives. Where joy is a valid reason for doing something. None of it because we need to, but because we understand how important, how vital, how fun it is to simply play, and even though the world we live in may not value it, that doesn't mean we can't.

Types of play

Did you know there is more than one kind of play? Perhaps as many as sixteen? Even though there are clear differences between make-believe games, board games, playing with clay and making a cereal-box theme park for your soft toys, I'd never really considered that there were different categories of play, nor that we each have our own preferences. Recognising these different types of play has shown me why I've felt disconnected from play for so long—I'd been stuck on the idea that it needed to look a particular way.

Dr Stuart Brown, founder of the US National Institute for Play, has developed categories of play that are vital not only to our development, but also to our mental health, our ability to form trust in our relationships, our emotional wellbeing, our job satisfaction and sense of empowerment as adults. Here's an incomplete list:

BODY PLAY AND MOVEMENT

What begins as a way for children to develop a spatial under-standing of themselves and the world around them becomes what Brown delightfully describes as 'a spontaneous desire to get out of the effects of gravity'.

Hanging upside down from monkey bars or learning a new dance teach us about the many different ways our body can move in relation to the world. This is what I'm looking for every time I get on a roller-coaster, it's what I enjoy most about my aikido lessons, and it's why I was lining up at the waterpark one sunny March morning, chatting with my brother-in-law about how playful we weren't.

OBJECT PLAY

This might be the most reminiscent of childhood—particularly if you loved playing with LEGO or building treehouses. As an adult, any kind of play that involves the manipulation of objects, building or designing can be considered object play.

I still get joy from a good pillow fort and, when the mood strikes, an hour or two spent playing around with my garden design. You might like creating a vision board or collage, building model train tracks, sewing doll clothes or decorating cakes.

~~~~~~~~~

IMAGINATIVE PLAY

As children, imaginative play offers us stories—the building blocks for how we learn about the world and our place in it. As adults it's a chance to work out our point of view, to try out different attitudes and character traits, to try on different costumes and see how the world feels when we wander through it in someone else's shoes for a while. For you, this might look like writing stories or joining a local theatre group or trying your hand at improv or dressing up as your favourite superhero at Halloween.

~~~~~~~~~

RITUAL PLAY

If you love playing games with set rules or structures—sports, chess, board games and the like—these are all considered ritual play. It's here, amid the rules and strategies, that we can learn how to interact and cooperate with others, uniting for a common goal or navigating the sometimes bruising waters of how to win and lose well. Interestingly, ritual play can also include spectating because the collective cheers count as play too, particularly when the enjoyment is more important than the outcome.

Ritual play might look like a weeks-long Monopoly game or joining the local Dungeons & Dragons club at the library. Many of the other types of play are more unstructured, so if you find that a little daunting it could be that ritual play is a more comfortable place to begin your exploration of play.

~~~~~~~~~

ROUGH AND TUMBLE PLAY

Tickling and tackling and running and rolling—it's believed that rough and tumble play is vital to children's development, but it's also beneficial to adults. Whether it's playing tug-of-war, a backyard game of soccer or throwing the kids around in the surf, the physical contact helps to calm our nervous system, while the exploration of personal space and boundaries helps us to develop trust.

~~~~~~~~~

LAUGHTER

There is something so satisfying about a big, meaty belly laugh. You know the kind that leaves your sides sore and tears running down your cheeks? While laughter is not a type of play in itself, the two are very closely linked and, what's more, laughter has been proven to have some incredible health benefits too. (Patch Adams was on to it, wasn't he?) Laughter is now being used as a complementary treatment for a variety of issues, ranging from stress to dementia, and has been shown to reduce anxiety levels. According to a broad review on the literature of the health benefits of laughter undertaken in 2005, it's been prescribed to cancer patients as a complementary treatment, to great effect, with improvements in immune function and pain thresholds, as well as a reduction in depressive symptoms and improved overall mood. A 2017 study by Irene Hatzipapas found that care workers working with HIV-affected families 'experienced more positive emotions, improved social relationships and improved ways of coping, as well as lower levels of anxiety, depression and stress' when prescribed laughter therapy.

Physically speaking, a big belly laugh can also mimic exercise, helping us to increase our heart rate and oxygen consumption, as well as improve our blood flow and cardiovascular health. In addition, social laughter (i.e. laughing with others) has been shown to elevate our pain thresholds, most likely due to the release of endorphins when we laugh as part of a group. For a low-cost,

There is no end to the
ways in which adults
can play; all you need
to do is figure out what
it looks like to you.
There's no right or
wrong way to play.

accessible care option with no known side effects, laughter is pretty powerful, so grab a friend, find a funny movie and have a chuckle.

How to play

It seems counter-intuitive, silly even, to offer a how-to for play but, as we've explored already, play doesn't come as naturally to many of us as it used to. The good news is there is no end to the ways in which adults can play; all you need to do is figure out what it looks like to you. What I find playful—a jigsaw puzzle, skiing or doodling, for example—might sound like torture to you. Similarly, Ben plays golf for fun and I'd just as soon watch paint dry. Some people have a preference for playing alone, while other people need company. There's no right or wrong way to play.

As a reformed non-playful person, I've found it useful to ask myself the somewhat clichéd question, 'What did I love playing as a child?' When I did I discovered a trove of childhood memories I could mine for inspiration. When the cushions on the floor weren't a mess, but my only hope of escaping a deadly lava field, or when a tunnel dug into the sand was a portal to another world. Making mud pies, playing Mouse Trap, or wielding lightsaber sticks. Blowing bubbles; painting rocks; long, slow walks spent inspecting neighbourhood flowers.

Brown calls this process 'writing a play history' and believes it is a key adults can use to unlock joy, happiness and satisfaction. Dig into your childhood and list as many play memories as you can. You might uncover clues about the kinds of activities you could do that can help reclaim your sense of play, not necessarily because the things you enjoyed then are the things you'll enjoy now, but because they could hold a clue for play you can adapt for your adult life. Or, you could just rediscover a love of Mouse Trap—who knows?

I have a distinct memory of playing with clothes pegs as a little kid. They were plastic and multicoloured: red, white and blue. I don't remember exactly what I was doing with them, but I remember being on the grass, hunched over a pile of these pegs, my mum nearby. Maybe I was sorting them or lining them up in a sequence, but whatever it was, I was completely immersed. Whenever I think about playing as a child, this is the first memory that comes to mind. Do I love playing with pegs now? No. But do I love immersive, quiet play—things like colouring or drawing or writing or jigsaw puzzles? Absolutely.

I also have a clear image of playing with a gloopy flour and water concoction with my sisters in the backyard. It was slimy and cool and I loved the sensation as I squeezed it through my fingers. (I also remember getting in trouble because we smeared the stuff all over the fence and left it there to bake in the summer heat—sorry, Mum xx.) I don't love playing with slime as an adult but I do love the sensation of gardening without gloves, digging in the dirt and mud until my hands are caked, and my nails are brown with soil. I love sitting at the beach, running my fingers across the sand, smoothing it out and making patterns, over and over again. I love playing with a little ball of clay, moulding and squashing and remoulding it, feeling it change under my fingers.

There are clues in your childhood that might point you towards a new, adult form of play that you hadn't considered before, or that you never thought of as play. Get curious, try one of them, letting go of any need to be good or to make progress or to complete something. Get playful and see where it leads you. See if you can remember what it felt like to be a kid, playing and exploring and trying new things just for the fun of it. If you find yourself feeling heavy at the idea of play, remember, none of this needs to be big or hard or overwhelming. In fact, I think that by practising play in small ways, by choosing to see even a few moments every day through the lens of play, you might be surprised at the impact it has on your worldview. Over time, as with so many of the acts of Small Care we're experimenting with, that decision to try morphs into action, those repeated actions become patterns, and those patterns gradually become the norm. Playing more regularly will allow you to become a person who plays, which is wonderful because I truly believe that the world needs more playful people.

Even though it's not possible to write an exhaustive list of ways to play, I wanted to offer a few ideas in case something here sparks a light in you. Keep in mind it's a list written from the perspective of an overthinking, over-earnest adult who still struggles to make laughter her default response and will probably never be quite as fun as Dad, but I hope there's something in here that feels like home.

IF YOU HAVE HALF A MINUTE

- Turn on your favourite song and dance around the house as you get ready in the morning.
- If you walk past a playground, stop and swing on the swings for a few minutes, or play at the park alongside your kids.
- Jump on a trampoline.
- Spend a few moments between meetings colouring in or doodling.
- Share a joke or a funny story with a colleague.

IF YOU HAVE HALF AN HOUR

- Take an online dance class—there are loads of great free classes on YouTube.
- Head to the beach for a bodysurf before work.
- String up a slackline between trees and spend some time trying to walk along it.
- Climb a tree.
- Practise handstands in a swimming pool.
- Take up skateboarding.
- Play dress-ups with your fancy clothes or costumes.
- Get sensory and make some goopy slime.
- Build a model aeroplane.

- Have a jigsaw puzzle out on the table and spend five minutes a day adding to it.
- Play a game of Jenga.
- Have a snowball fight.
- Write a limerick about someone you know.
- Tell your kids a story at bedtime, or read one out loud, using different voices and accents for the characters.
- Build a snowman.
- Play with your pets.

IF YOU HAVE HALF A DAY OR MORE

- Head to a ropes course, or go abseiling.
- Grab your surfboard and get out in the waves.
- Go skiing (water, downhill or cross-country).
- Find a snorkelling spot and go explore.
- Head to an amusement park and ride the biggest roller-coaster you can find.
- Sign yourself up for an open-mic comedy night and try stand-up (or just go and watch).
- Join a local improv or theatre group.

CHAPTER 8

rest

Is there not a space between

the tumult and the pulse?

A place we may rest,

quiet the noise, the inner voice.

Sink gently into being

air and blood and flesh and bone

Being here, being now

Only being. Home.

Everything we've explored in the book so far has led us to this point.

All the connecting and listening and noticing, all the time spent in awe and nature and wonder, the kindness, creativity and play, has prepared us for this experiment—one that might prove to be the most difficult yet.

What is this difficult experiment, you ask?

It's nothing.

. . .

No, really, it's nothing.

. . .

I don't mean it's insignificant, I mean it's actually nothing. *Doing* nothing.

You know. Chilling. Vegging. Mooching. Basking. Hanging. Sweet Fanny Adams.

I'm talking about delicious, syrupy idleness. An idea that many of us have a tortured relationship with, given its connotations of laziness, luxury, guilt and privilege.

This is hardly surprising, of course, given productivity hacks and leaning in and finding a side gig are now part of the curriculum of modern life. We all know that hustlers prosper while slackers lag and when you combine this with the age-old idioms that tell us we should *Never put off until tomorrow what we can do today*, and *Idle hands are the devil's workshop* . . . Well, things start to get serious. Add to that the worn-out adage that *Only boring people get bored*, we understandably cram life full of relentless activity and consumption, trying to stave off that nothingness, trying to keep the boredom at bay, trying to prove our worth.

We buy stuff, we eat stuff, we read reams of information on our screens, we watch hundreds of hours of television, we listen to podcasts, we search for the hole-shaped thing that will plug the gap in our lives, that might just allow us to feel content. The thing that could just be the key to unlocking a sense of self-worth and maybe, just maybe, allow us to stop for a moment. The good news, I guess, is that there is literally no end to the things we can do and consume in order to alleviate boredom. We could fill up several lifetimes with those efforts if we wanted to.

Yet, we also crave downtime. In pre-Covid times we craved it because the pace of our lives was brutal and our brains were screaming for a reprieve and now, as the world continues to change due to Covid, I believe many of us crave downtime either because the overwhelming nature of pandemic-related news, rolling public health updates and concern for family and friends leaves us burnt out and exhausted, or because lockdowns remind us what it felt like to stay home, to rest, to actively avoid making plans, to potter around our homes. Perhaps they also showed us that caring for ourselves and those around us can be as simple (and as difficult) as staying in.

So, yes, I think we have a tortured relationship with idleness. We find the idea of doing nothing deeply uncomfortable and incredibly attractive, a shameful, exciting thing. We are apologetically delighted by it. A weekend with no plans stretches out in front of us and we can barely contain our excitement before asking ourselves what we should fill it with, as it would be such a shame to waste it doing nothing.

'You're predisposed to idleness,' said Ben one May morning, not unkindly, as I wandered the veggie garden with a cup of coffee. I'd told him I was going out for five minutes but, as often happens, time stretched out as I slowly moved around the beds, inspecting the broccoli and kale and cauliflower seedlings, turning the leaves over, searching their soft undersides for the tiny, white, full-stop eggs of the cabbage moth and scraping them off with my thumbnail, and winding the seeking tendrils of my new pea shoots towards the twine and timber frame I had made a few weekends earlier.

It's no surprise to anyone who knows me that I love these quiet moments. Over the years I've explored and experimented with slowing down and as a result have discovered so much joy in the peaceful minutes tucked in among the folds of a full life. I will advocate endlessly for the benefits of finding these pockets of slow in our days, and still I found myself unsure whether my husband telling me I was predisposed to idleness should leave me feeling offended or proud because, at least the way I saw it, I wasn't being idle. I was moving around the garden, bending and weeding and tending and observing. Sure, I was doing it all slowly, not adhering to any agenda or trying to tick items off my to-do list, but it wasn't lazy. Was it?

Perhaps the issue is that we don't really know how to define idleness. Is the only way to be idle to do literally nothing? Or is it doing things at a relaxed pace? Is scrolling our phones an example of idleness, or wandering the garden or watching TV or reading a book or going for a walk?

To me idleness speaks of doing nothing at all, but the truth is that modern life has not equipped us for the act of literally doing nothing. Even when we think that's what we're doing, often it's not the case. We might physically be still as we scroll our phones, read the news, catch up on the latest episode of our favourite show or listen to a podcast, and we might convince ourselves that we're doing nothing. But those things aren't nothing.

Idleness is defined by the Merriam-Webster dictionary as 'a lack of action or activity', but we don't have a framework for doing nothing

Modern life has
not equipped us
for the act of
literally doing
nothing.

and we don't have many examples of it to model ourselves on. We feel the need to always be producing or consuming and, as we've seen throughout this book, both of these modes of doing have a place in our lives.

There is a space in between though, where we can sit, simply being. There is a space into which we can expand and think our thoughts and live in our rich but largely ignored inner lives for a moment, where we can reflect and delve and ponder. The time spent in this in-between is not wasted—though by today's consume/produce standards it may appear to be—it is vital in learning how to settle into ourselves, to find some contentment and self-awareness, and only through time spent there will we ever free ourselves from the relentless need to *do*. Learning to live a part of every day in the in-between is how the things we do take on meaning and importance. It's where we work out how we feel and why, it's when we make discoveries about who we are and who we're becoming. Learning to live a part of every day in the in-between is how we change our lives.

The Western world doesn't operate in a way that makes idleness easy. In fact, you might need to tap into your inner rebel in order to do so because learning to embrace idleness requires a certain amount of defiance, a desire to push back against the status quo a little because, really, is there anything more counter-cultural than joyfully doing nothing at all? We know society demands activity of us, if not at work or through our outputs on social media or in maintaining our homes or ensuring that even our pottering is productive (if you're not tidying and organising your house à la *The Home Edit* then can you even call it a weekend?) then at the very least in a pre-approved list of socially acceptable, commodified self-care rituals. Turns out the only kind of idleness we're really encouraged to partake in is the capitalist kind: spa days, Netflix binges, takeaway dinners, health retreats, face masks. These are all welcome because presumably we'll be paying for all of these things with *money* that we've made *working* because we are productive members of society. And, well, money makes the world go 'round after all, doesn't it?

The status quo is clearly not working for us. The confusing mix of guilty relief many of us felt on lockdown is evidence of this. It shouldn't have taken a devastating pandemic for so many of us to recognise how much we need downtime, but it did. It was the first time many of us stopped to think about just how much of our time and energy goes into doing all the things that we 'should' be doing, and as we stopped and became acclimatised to less activity, many of us found something unexpected there.

I was amazed, and quite honestly buoyed, by the conversations I found myself having with people during the early days of lockdown. Conversations about the environment, about social welfare policies, about mental health and the need to prioritise services for those of us living with mental illness, about funding public hospitals, about what constitutes an essential worker, about the immense pressure put on our teachers and frontline healthcare workers, about media bias and disinformation. It was as though stepping back from the regular rush of our day-to-day lives freed up space to think a little more, to notice the world around us, to reflect on what's been happening in front of our eyes for years but that we only had time to see once the blinkers of endless activity were removed.

When we're busy fixing and working and choring and maintaining and waiting for the day when we can enjoy our much-awaited rest, we don't get the chance to ask, could it be that this relentless pace serves another purpose, one beyond relentless productivity? Busy, overwhelmed people don't usually spend time questioning the system they live in. When we're trying to keep our heads above water, we're not looking at social justice, we're not asking how much our lowest-paid workers are receiving, or why clothes and home goods are so cheap or where all of our plastic goes when we throw it away. We can't, we're too busy. At weekends we're painting and gardening and brunching and drinking and socialising. Our pace of life has been robbing us of the curiosity and care required to change the world.

So, if we're so entrenched in the cult of doing, is it even possible to learn how to stop? Yes, but the irony is this: it's going to take work.

Slow down everyone, you're moving too fast

I like to think I'm pretty good at taking things slowly, at least some of the time. I realise that I'm not quite as good at doing nothing at all, so as I began working on this chapter, I decided to conduct an experiment to see what my baseline comfort level was when it came to being idle. I decided to dedicate fifteen minutes to pure idleness by simply lying on my bed one Saturday afternoon. No reading, no meditating, no nothing. I'd leave my phone in the kitchen, my book on the bedside table. I'd simply lie down and see what would happen.

You might think that sounds easy. I thought it would be easy. Let me just say that when I first read a statistic from researchers at the University of Virginia that said two-thirds of men and more than a quarter of women studied would prefer to self-administer electric shocks than sit alone with their thoughts for fifteen minutes, I thought it was absurd. Now I kind of understand.

My experiment began when I told my family I was having a rest, closed the bedroom door and lay down on my bed. I wriggled around to get comfy. I breathed, and then I sighed, wriggled some more and then I waited.

After what felt like at least fifteen minutes I checked my watch. Not even two minutes had passed. So, I waited some more.

Soon my body itched with the desire to do something, anything. My thoughts got really loud and really messy, shouting over each other, vying for my attention. I felt like my heart rate increased. But instead of giving in and getting up, I lay there. I looked out the window, I stared at the ceiling, I listened with distant ears to the comings and goings of the rest of the house. The dogs barking, the kids playing, my husband rattling around in the kitchen. I didn't engage with any of it. I was working really hard on doing nothing.

Gradually, I stopped wriggling. My thoughts stopped shouting. I softened into the space I'd carved out. I stared at the ceiling some more and thought my thoughts, letting them come and go as I dipped in and out of memories and felt out the fullness of ideas, with no planning, no direction, no agenda.

There was no big moment of realisation, only a slight melting into the in-between, that space that exists between consuming and creating, between input and output, the space that offered me the ability to simply be.

All up I lay on my bed for nearly an hour and realised when I stood back up that I felt different—decompressed, as though someone had grabbed me by the feet and hung me upside down for a little while, letting the stiff, tight disks of my spine lengthen out until I felt airy and spacious. It took some work to get there, mind you, but it's an experiment I'd encourage you to try, and one I've found myself going back to over the months since.

La dolce far niente

At this point I'd love to introduce you to the Italian concept of *la dolce far niente*, which means 'the sweetness of doing nothing'. It can look like lots of different things—napping in the afternoon, or people-watching from an outdoor seat at the local coffee shop, or idly wandering your neighbourhood with nowhere in particular to go, nothing in particular to do. *La dolce far niente* is as beneficial to our wellbeing as it is appealing, but here's why I'm not going to suggest you dive into it headfirst. We're so results-driven, conditioned to value productivity, that even our efforts at self-care and wellbeing need to be quantifiably good. (Nowhere to go? How will I know when I arrive? Nothing to do? How will I know when I've *done* it?) For many of us, stepping into delicious idleness won't come easily, so I've devised a (slightly tongue-in-cheek but also hopefully helpful) training plan to help you build your 'do-nothing' muscles. It might seem silly, or perhaps you're already someone who knows how to be idle, in which case, go on with your bad self. But many among us are not so well equipped to dive right into doing nothing and it's for those of us who struggle that I've created the Official Learn to Do Nothing Training Guide. (Follow these four simple steps and you too will be doing nothing like a champ in no time!)

Perhaps you think that sounds paradoxical: having to work at doing nothing. However, when the norm is to be constantly producing or consuming, doing nothing needs to be an event, one you can plan for, train for, apply yourself to. And, just like any other training, over time you'll find that you'll build the muscle memory and strength that allows you to slip in and out of idleness far more easily.

Let me start by saying that there are times when the sweetness of doing nothing is a pretty terrible idea. Staring idly while driving—terrible idea. While presenting to the board—terrible idea. While operating on a patient or serving a customer or handing out awards at school assembly—terrible idea. But that doesn't mean we don't have other opportunities to embrace *la dolce far niente* for a minute. Even when we're busy.

STAGE 1—BABY STEPS

Set aside a few minutes and dedicate the time to the practice of doing nothing. Ideally, you'll do this every day, but since you're just starting out, find whatever time you can and go from there. You might nominate the five minutes you spend sitting in your car outside school pick-up or set your alarm for five minutes earlier every morning. Maybe you sit in the park on your lunchbreak, lie on your bed, turn up to your yoga class a few minutes early—it doesn't matter where the time comes from, just find a way to carve out a few minutes from your day and commit to spending them doing absolutely nothing.

Once you've set that time aside, make use of your Unplug tool and turn your phone off, or at least put it on silent and set it out of your line of sight. (If you're worried about going over time, or constantly checking your progress, feel free to set a timer for a few minutes.) You are allowed to take these few moments and, I can almost guarantee you, whatever the pinging, buzzing notifications signify can wait until you finish. Then, take a moment to get comfy. Wriggle around and find a restful position to sit in. You might even want to channel your cat or dog, the way they stretch and move when they sit down and prepare to rest, adjusting and readjusting until they're ready for stillness.

Now comes the hard part. You need to just . . . stop. Be still. Settle into your body and breathe. Don't feel like you need to meditate or be mindful of anything, you're in training for doing nothing, and nothing means nothing—no agenda, no reason. Nothing at all.

You might feel itchy or jittery at first. Perhaps your thoughts will get noisy. Now is probably the time your brain serves up a list of all the other things you should be doing, running through your to-do list. Ignore it.

You might want to reach for your phone. Don't. It can wait.

Sit with any discomfort that arises. By all means, recognise it, acknowledge it, but don't engage with it. A friendly wave, an 'I'll come and see you in a minute' half-smile, but let it wait as you continue to simply *be*. Revel in the experience of *being*. This may or may not feel pleasant.

Then, when your time is up, give your fingers and toes a wiggle, take a deep breath, and move on with your day.

Try this each day for a week and observe how you feel when you do it. Is there any change in the way you approach your practice? Are you sitting for longer? Are you feeling more or less agitated? Are you learning how to acknowledge your thoughts while also leaving them alone?

STAGE 2—SITTING WITH YOUR INNER LIFE

As your 'do nothing' muscles continue to strengthen, you're going to extend the length of time you're in training. You can add five more minutes to your idle time or find a second window throughout your day. (Just a heads-up, sitting on the toilet can count, as can waiting for the bus, queueing at the farmers' market or waiting for a friend to meet you at the pub.) Wherever you decide to practise, go through the same process each time and continue to observe your reactions as you sit (stand, lie) with them.

You might find that this is when your brain starts serving up scene after scene of memories you'd rather forget—the dumb thing you said in a meeting, the horrible phone call you made, the way you screwed up a problem at home—it's okay. One of the reasons so many of us work hard to avoid boredom in the first place is because our inner lives often feel uncomfortable. The regrets, the mistakes, the foot-in-mouth moments, they all bubble up to the surface when we stop cramming more in. These thoughts are part of our inner lives, and learning how to be with them, learning how to acknowledge them without reacting, is an important part of developing stillness. Let them float in and out of your head and continue to simply be.

~~~~~~~

STAGE 3—MEANDERING

If you're feeling strong, try taking your practice on the move, either in addition to or instead of practising in private. Go for a brief walk and leave your phone at home. (If you can't, at least keep it in your pocket and have your ears bud-free. It's incredibly hard for us to practise doing nothing when listening to music or a podcast.) Try listening to the sounds around you instead or let thoughts roll around in your head as you practise doing nothing with them.

You might find it difficult at first to acknowledge that this isn't for exercise—it's not necessary to get your heart rate up or walk a particular distance. As strange as it may seem, this is simply a practice in idle wandering, much like a flâneur. Nowhere to go, nowhere to be. You can walk with your thoughts, you can walk without them, you can spend time paying attention to the buildings and trees and people and animals you see, or not. You've now reached the meandering stage of your training!

~~~~~~~

STAGE 4—LA DOLCE FAR NIENTE

Try expanding your practice to thirty minutes at least once a week. Can you take a longer walk? Are you able to use your commute as your longer practice? Perhaps your kids have dance practice or karate lessons; instead of spending that time doing the groceries or

sink gently into being

catching up on news or racing home to get dinner on before racing back to pick them up, could you sit in the car for thirty minutes and practise doing nothing? Maybe you can shut yourself in your bedroom, letting your family know that you're having alone time, or wait until the kids are in bed and take a bath. Maybe you could go somewhere in nature where you can just sit and be. A beach, a river, a lake or a lookout, a quiet bush track or a paddock.

What you'll discover after practising for a while is that your 'do nothing' muscles know how to proceed, allowing thoughts to wander and eyes to land and move on. You will gradually be able to resist the urge to scroll, write or create with remarkably little effort. You are now ready to idle at will. Congratulations!

Over time, you can also begin practising at other times during the day, when you're folding the laundry or checking the mail or walking from the train station to your office, for example. Once you're equipped with the skill of idling, everyday tasks and pockets of your day offer opportunities to find stillness, even if you're technically in motion. This is where *la dolce far niente* starts really making sense, where you realise that not every moment of the day needs to have productive goals attached to it, and you become content to move slowly and idly. You can call it mind-wandering or daydreaming if you want, but whatever you call it, this is when the benefits of idleness really start to make themselves known in your life.

Perhaps that all sounds very nice to you (or perhaps not), but the question remains, how can doing nothing help you care for yourself and others?

Idleness allows us to decompress from the relentless noise of modern life, providing an opportunity to recalibrate to a baseline of stillness where the ability to simply *be* for a moment does not result in boredom but in peace: relief in the quiet.

That's what doing nothing offers. That's what mind-wandering and daydreaming offers: a counterweight to the heaviness of a hectic world. We shouldn't need big impressive reasons to adopt a little idleness into our days when the very joy of it stems from the fact that we see the things that need doing and we choose to stop for a moment anyway.

So it feels almost wrong to follow this up with more reasons to practise doing nothing, but the truth is that idleness offers us a great deal more than just recalibration.

When we're in everyday working, planning, goal-setting, decision-making mode—the mode we spend the majority of our waking hours operating in—certain parts of the brain are more active than others. This is often called our 'executive function', otherwise known as the management system of the brain. When we're dealing with lots of inputs, when we're stressed, when there's a lot of noise and notifications and hustle and bustle, our executive function helps us to navigate the sheer volume of information and stimulus. It helps us to pay attention, organise, plan, prioritise, regulate our emotions, start tasks and stay focused on them. Getting through a day without utilising our executive function would be incredibly tough, but while we're in this planning, doing, decision-making mode, there is another network in our brain that can't function effectively. It's called the 'default mode network' and it's where imagination, creativity and problem-solving happen. It's also where we make connections between disparate ideas and where solutions to long-held, nagging problems come from. Since the early 2000s, neuroscientists have been exploring the theory that this default mode network only becomes active when we're at rest or when we're doing something like daydreaming, mind-wandering, or completing a task we're so familiar with that we don't really need to think much about it. In a study published by the National Academy of Science in

2012, brain scans showed that the default mode network activates when people are at rest, but not sleeping (i.e. when we're 'just thinking'). Scans also showed that when a person is given a specific task to do, the network seems to deactivate, replaced by activity in different parts of the brain.

Essentially that means that while we live our fast-paced, ever-active, stressful, noisy, permanently tech-connected lives, we are unable to use our brains to their best problem-solving and creative ability, which means we could be leaving our best ideas on the table. By staying endlessly active we're doing ourselves, our families, friends, communities, towns and cities a disservice.

Right now there are hugely complex problems facing society—how to create new, more equitable economic models in a post-Covid world, how to arrest global warming, how to transfer previously coal and fossil fuel reliant economies to a just, low-carbon future—and if we're all too busy *doing* to stop, to slow down our brains, to shift into that default mode network, we're robbing ourselves of our best, world-changing ideas right when we need them most.

Consider the last time you solved a problem or came up with a solution to something that had been bugging you. Were you working on it directly? Sweating over the ins and outs of it, or were you doing something else? Sweeping the floor or peeling potatoes or staring out the window? That's no accident. That's our brains shifting into the default mode network. You've no doubt seen it play out in movies or TV shows because scriptwriters are familiar with the phenomenon. The character is struggling to solve a problem, probably a big one. She toils, she grimaces, she pulls her hair off her face, she looks harried and stressed. She sighs and sits back, deflated and stuck. She looks out the window or picks up the random trinket on her desk or simply stares absently. And then! All of a sudden! She sits up straight as though she's just been zapped with a jolt of electricity, and a smile of recognition lights up her face. That's it! She's got it. Hermione Granger (or Eloise Bridgerton or Katniss Everdeen or insert your protagonist here) has the idea that will save the day and she races off to brew the potion and Act 3 of the film can start.

So, how do we actually access this magical, life-changing, world-shifting default mode network in real life? We slow down. We build idle, unstructured, daydreaming, mind-wandering time into our days. We stare out the window, we do mundane tasks with no additional noise, we sit on the train and do nothing, we go for a walk for no reason other than to wander, we sit in a coffee shop and simply watch the comings and goings of the people around us. We pull a chair into the sun for a moment of contemplative nothingness.

We embrace idle time; we adopt *la dolce far niente* and we stop seeing quiet moments as empty vessels into which we must pour productivity. Instead, we learn to recognise that the real gift of those empty moments is the space they give us to expand, to get to know ourselves and connect the dots.

And if we practise the art of doing nothing at all, we will find that these moments of idle meandering are plentiful, if we're willing to look for them.

IF YOU HAVE HALF A MINUTE

- When you wake in the morning, take thirty seconds to simply lie still and listen to the sounds around you.

- Let your mind wander as you complete a mundane task, like washing dishes or weeding the garden.

- Stare out the window between phone calls.

- When you feel bored, resist the urge to pick up your phone and, instead, listen to your thoughts.

- Look at a photo or memento on your desk and see what memories it conjures.

- Stand in the sun and feel its warmth on your back.

IF YOU HAVE HALF AN HOUR

- Sit in a bar or coffee shop and people-watch, eavesdrop and let your mind wander.

- Take a nap.

- Lie on your bed and do nothing.

- Make a cup of tea and sit outside to drink it—no phone, no book, just you, your tea and your thoughts.

- Watch the light travel across your living room wall as the sun sets.

- Play an album in full and simply sit and listen to it.
- Lie on the grass and watch the clouds.
- Light a fire and watch the flames.
- Sit companionably in silence with someone you love.

IF YOU HAVE HALF A DAY OR MORE

- Take a long, meandering walk around your neighbourhood, with no destination in mind and no phone.
- Set up a picnic blanket at the park and spend a few hours aimlessly—eating, reading, playing or snoozing.
- Read a collection of poetry and allow yourself time between each poem to think about the words, the imagery, the themes of each piece.
- Head to the coast and wander the rockpools.
- Go camping and take no entertainment with you (no books, no card games, etc.) just rely on your own imagination and see where it takes you.

CHAPTER 9

healing

When your heart is dull and ashy
with the relentless grit of the road,
When your throat is parched and rasping
And your voice a dusty ghost
When your shoulders are pulled to the earth
by ropes that strip your flesh to the bone

May you be blessed, my friend,
with ears to hear this secret
speaking confidently
in your very bones.
May you be blessed, my friend,
with heart to be courageous
in sharing this offering
with your road-dusted companions.

May you be blessed, my friend,

with love enough

to make yourself heard

above the noise and tumult.

Hear this whisper.

Pass it down the line.

Rest easy.

Your heart will be restored

your voice will return

your flesh be made whole.

But not on the road, my friend.

For now, we turn home.

I didn't leave this chapter to the end because it's the least important— just the opposite really.

I always hoped the road would lead us here and, now that we've arrived, I want the landscape we're about to explore to be fresh in your mind when you close this book. I want you to remember that what we talk about in this chapter is an option *that's available to you.*

We forget we are not machines. We forget we are living, breathing beings that are part of nature—just like the trees and the butterflies and the rivers. So used to productivity and efficiency and uniformity and push-button convenience and instant gratification and binary thinking that we forget what it means to take time, to care.

Similar to the plants and animals and cycles and seasons of the natural world we're part of, we also experience periods of growth and periods of fallowness. We have times of great productivity and times where we turn inward, quiet and still, in order to gather the energy we need for the coming spring. We would not expect roses to bloom year-round, or nests to always be full of nestlings, so we should not expect ourselves to push through our own cycles of growth and dormancy. Yet we do. We tell ourselves that we just need to keep showing up, keep striving, keep moving forward. That we'll rest some other time. That after this week things should really quieten down. And still, we're surprised when it falls apart. When we throw our backs out and spend a few days bed-bound on painkillers. When we come down with a vicious flu and need two weeks off to recuperate. When our mental health takes a nosedive. When our relationship falls apart. When loneliness threatens to drag us under. When our health reaches crisis point. It still shocks us, this reminder that we are, in fact, human. We forget we are not machines.

Nor are we binary creatures, easily categorised into one kind or the other. We are complex, multi-layered and ever-evolving, but the world we live in prefers us to be easily labelled and static. With or against. Red or blue. Yes or no. Pro or anti. To riff on Walt Whitman, we contain multitudes, you and I. Inside our complex beings is enough space to hold numerous truths at once, some of which might seem to contradict each other at first glance. Surely, we think, don't these wishy-washy shades of grey make us weak? Flaky? Liars or fence-sitters or hypocrites? No. They simply make us human. The kind of human who can be both depressed and grateful. Sad and hopeful. Engaged and exhausted. A human who can love someone deeply and not want to be near them. Who cares wholeheartedly about something and needs to step back from it, who needs to heal from it.

This chapter is your permission slip to experience those seeming contradictions, to own the messy, delightful, liberating, confusing complexity that is holding two conflicting ideas within yourself at the same time: specifically, your capacity to care and your need to step back. Because you are allowed to take time away. You are allowed to create boundaries. You are allowed to focus on healing when you get tired, or sick, or burnt out. More than that, you are allowed to focus on healing *before* you get tired, or sick, or burnt out. This doesn't mean you're hiding. It doesn't mean you don't care about the important things, or that you've hardened yourself against them, it means you care so much about them that you need to take time away, so that you may continue to care.

For years, I've heard rumours of a particular breed of human unicorn (maybe you've heard of them too?) that has no difficulty whatsoever in stepping back and prioritising their own healing. They happily acknowledge their limitations and take action to protect themselves from burnout. Now, I know it sounds unlikely, and I personally have never met one, but I have it on good authority that these unicorns do indeed exist. If you know one, or if you *are* one, then feel free to share some of that magic with the rest of us. If, however, you're a regular human like me, who struggles to prioritise your own healing, please know that you're not alone, and please know that everyone (probably even unicorns) will at some time in their lives, burn out. And you know what? It's okay. It's life, and sometimes, my friend, it simply asks too much of us. Activists burn out. Parents burn out. Students burn out. Carers burn out. Optimists and artists and teachers and builders—we will all experience times when the balance of energy out versus energy in is too uneven, when our Big Care outweighs the Small, maybe by a lot. Some people experience this as physical illness while others go through periods of depression or anxiety. For some it feels like falling into numbness—a not-caring that feels frightening—while others feel sad and tired. It can affect your health, sleep, energy, appetite, friendships, work and every other area of your life. I'm quite sure whoever you are, whatever your life looks like, you've experienced this feeling of being *done*, over it, ready to throw in the towel or to run away. Wanting nothing more than to step back and regain some space in which you can heal, only to be brought up short by the guilt, the inner voice telling you that you don't deserve rest, that other people have it harder and you should just toughen up and keep swimming.

It's unfortunate then, that outside the modern-day conversations around 'me time' and self-care (and their associated problems), there's not really any broad discussion happening about what it could look like if stepping back felt permissible.

We've already seen how the notions of idleness and rest are hard to adapt to, which begs the question: what *can* we do? How do we explain to our friends why their messages are going unanswered or to our colleagues that we need to take unscheduled time off? How do we pass the baton of our community work to our fellow members or tell our kids we are capital 'D' Done and need time alone, just for a little while?

In her book *All Good Things*, Sarah Turnbull briefly mentions a Tahitian word that wraps all of this up in three little letters. *Fiu* is a simple word (perfectly and aptly pronounced 'phew') that neatly sums up the myriad complex experiences of what we might call burnout. And while I love the shorthand of a single word, what I love even more is that in Tahiti, it appears that *fiu* is an acceptable, one-word explanation for absence from work, life or family. *Fiu* can be offered as justification for work absences, unplanned store closures or cancelled social engagements, and it goes unquestioned.

'Sorry boss, I'm not coming in this week. I'm *fiu*.'

'No worries, take care. See you soon.'

I mean, *can you even imagine*? Can you imagine saying to your boss (or partner or friend), 'Actually, I'm really struggling right now and need some time away, I'll be back soon,' and for them to just *accept* it, no questions asked?

I'm trying to think of equivalent social contracts in Western cultures, where we feel able to opt out for a bit. Perhaps in certain situations, certain relationships or workplaces something similar exists, but there aren't too many broadly applicable circumstances where I see it working because, while we may not be machines, we all spend a lot of time thinking we need to be.

I've done it many times myself. When things get stressful or difficult, I slip into robot mode and try my best to just push through until things get better. Every morning I weigh up the necessities of the day—food, work, logistics—and go about the mechanical process of getting up, getting dressed, making lunches, logging on to my computer to start work, showing up to meetings and appointments, buying groceries, cooking dinner, cleaning, laundry. To someone on the outside it might appear that I'm Doing Fine because I'm still keeping up with all the things I should be. I'm clean and presentable and smile at the appropriate moments and turn up when I need to. I usually even tell myself I'm Doing Fine for the same reasons and fully expect that I will continue to grind through.

Until I can't. This doesn't happen frequently of course, but often enough to recognise the pattern, the one where my body taps me on the shoulder with a reminder (a cold, an injury, a stomach bug) that I am human. If I continue to ignore these polite taps, they usually get ruder and more aggressive until BAM, I can't pretend anymore. I get laid up, laid out, forced to acknowledge, even temporarily, that I am definitely not a machine and am left to deal with the fallout.

No doubt, this is an experience most of us have some familiarity with, so what are we losing when we let this behaviour steal from us? When we turn into robots, what we don't have is joy. Or awe. Or long, precious moments given to beauty or music or laughter or tears of gratitude. We don't have the heartfelt conversations and afternoons where time stretches out and means *more*. We lose curiosity, peace and sheer delight at the tiniest of noticings. We're no longer aware of the lightness of heart that comes from acknowledging and being acknowledged by a stranger or the warm feeling in our chests that radiates in the company of kindness. The expansive pride found in making something and the giddy gladness of deep belly laughs are gone. These are the golden flecks in life, and these are what we lose when we stay too long in machine mode. This is why we need to step back from things we care about sometimes, without guilt. To get perspective, we need to see the forest *and* the trees.

We need to give ourselves permission to be human, to heal. But, in this, the real world, what does that look like? I'd love to suggest a global uptake of *fiu*—where we all sign the social contract that says, 'I will tell you if I'm struggling, I will take the time I need to heal, and when the shoe is on the other foot, I will allow you the space and time.' Considering, however, that this book is grounded in realistic ideas, I instead encourage you not to wait for someone else to create the social contract you're craving. Write your own. Look to your immediate circles and find someone to talk to about all of this with. It may be a friend, your partner, siblings or a close colleague, anyone who you think might just get it. Introduce them to the idea of *fiu*, laugh about how it would probably never fly, and then say something like, 'But can you imagine if it did? We should come up with our own word—a signal that we need the other to step in for us. Create our own little tag-team.' See what happens when you make an intentional choice to create the kind of support you need. See how you feel even just having the conversation, imagining a different way.

Yes, this applies even if you're the only doctor in town, the only parent to your child, or the only qualified person in the room. Stepping back is not the same as stepping away from your responsibilities, so let that guilt go. Consider instead, what would happen if you kept pushing, kept ignoring the warning signs and burnt all the way out, if you were left physically or emotionally or mentally incapable of showing up for those responsibilities? How devastating or difficult would that be for the work/cause/people you serve and love? I'm not asking you that question to make you feel guilty, I'm asking in the hope that it provides perspective that can be hard to find when you're deep in machine mode. To recognise what's at stake. If we don't create opportunity for regular reprieve, we risk it all.

Let's normalise the
idea of stepping back.
Learn to recognise it
as another facet of
care. One that will
allow us to recharge,
heal, rethink and reset
our expectations.

Let's normalise the idea of stepping back, as opposed to stepping (or running) away. Learn to recognise it as another facet of care. One that will allow us to recharge, heal, rethink and reset our expectations, and return to ourselves, our relationships, our communities, grounded, well and ready to show up in big and small ways. First though, we need to learn how to loosen our grip.

Stop should-ing all over yourself

As a starting point, let's check the language we use when we talk about why we can't stop. We say should, have to, need to, ought to. As a card-carrying Adult, there's a lot of responsibility to shoulder, undoubtedly, but we also tend to pick up assumptions and add them to the load as we go. We take on the maximum burden that could ever be expected of us, and then add a little more. Perhaps these shoulds we carry have been handed down as family norms or societal expectations. Maybe those who passed them on to us in the first place are simply giving to us what was given to them, making the status quo a little more deeply ingrained every time. Regardless, it's time we start questioning. It's time we get to know our inner rebel a little more and ask what they think of these loads we carry around.

Write a list of the shoulds you're holding on to. Ask yourself how you feel about each of them. Identify one thing on that list and picture yourself picking it up and sticking it in a cupboard. Shut the door. Leave it there. Live without its weight and mass for a while and see how it feels. This might mean giving yourself permission to drop some balls along the way. Try not to worry too much. Social commitments, a tidy desk, inbox zero, homemade lunchbox treats, organising the school fundraiser . . . Put one of them down for a while, and when the shoulds that accompany it start back up in your ear, stick them in the cupboard too.

Pay attention to how you feel once you've reclaimed the space this should once occupied. Luxuriate in it for a while. You might find yourself unwilling to pick it back up again, or with an unbridled desire to put more shoulds in the cupboard, which might make your inner rebel very, very happy.

Set boundaries

Now for the tricky part: making sure the space you reclaim doesn't get filled with other shoulds. Enter, boundaries.

We often think about creating healthy boundaries as something we do for external parts of our life—work, friends, kids, partners— but less so for our inner lives. We'll set aside time for a weekly family dinner or an annual girls' weekend and, because it's important, we defend it. Time to step back and heal ourselves is just as, if not more, important, but we're far less likely to create and protect these kinds of boundaries. Maybe it's a self-worth thing, or a guilt thing, I don't know, but if you're concerned that the space you reclaim by dropping some shoulds will be taken over by new ones, it's important to ask yourself what kind of space you require and then create boundaries within which you're free to do the healing you need.

Try writing a list (yes, another one!) of ten things, just for you, that make you feel better in some way; things that leave you rested, appreciated, grounded, delighted, understood, heard, loved, strong or worthy. Maybe it's daily meditation, or a weekly solo bike ride, or monthly therapy sessions. What do these things look like for you? What's involved in each of them? Is there something small you can do every day, and a larger one you can do every month? Once you've nominated one, schedule time for it, just like you would a coffee with a friend. Whether that means getting up five minutes earlier or turning your phone to Do Not Disturb at 8 pm every night, watching one less episode of a TV show or leaving the office for your lunchbreak most days, it's important to remember that our boundaries around healing are not going to build (or defend) themselves. That's something we need to learn to do ourselves.

Support

That's not to say we need to do it *all* ourselves. In fact, if we're going to normalise the idea of stepping back when we need to, we need to practise asking for help. To do so is not evidence of failure, it's an acknowledgement that you're feeling the pressure. It's showing vulnerability and that can be scary, but it's also brave, and an invitation to others to consider their own tendency to push through. Admitting you're human invites honesty, understanding, self-awareness and insight, in yourself, yes, but also in the person you're sharing with. Asking for help paves the way for more of these moments of honesty, more assumptions being questioned and more burdens being placed in cupboards. This is how we create shifts in the status quo: one conversation, one admission, one moment of awkward, scary bravery at a time. Take a breath, toss that pebble and watch the ripples spread.

Asking for help looks different for everyone, and it will vary throughout different stages of life. Perhaps it might mean asking for a referral to a psychologist or sending an email to a friend letting them know you're not feeling great. You could call a mental health hotline for a chat or ring your mum and have a good cry. Ask if your kids can have a sleepover at a friend's house. Tell your boss you need more support on the project you're struggling with. You don't need to carry it all alone.

While it's enough to simply acknowledge your need to step back, the benefits of prioritising your healing are also powerful and transformative, and can result in:

- **reduced levels of cortisol, or stress hormone**
- reduced heart rate and blood pressure
- **increased sense of belonging and purpose**
- increased sense of happiness
- **being better able to manage periods of stress**
- improved sleep
- **increased energy levels**
- improved brain function
- **increased circulation.**

All of which is lovely. But how can we use this little bit of space we've created and defended? How can we heal (particularly if week-long health retreats are out of reach)? First, ask yourself what you need more of. Is it rest or silence or orgasms or laughter or time in the ocean? Meandering or yoga or bike riding or birdwatching or bingeing *Outlander*? If you don't know, or if it all feels too big or out of reach, there are little things you can do that offer surprisingly potent benefits.

~~~~~~~~~

BREATHE

We do it thousands of times a day, but how often do we focus on breathing, really? One of the simplest things we can do to create a moment of healing in our day is to learn how to breathe well. Which seems kind of silly considering we all know how to do it, or rather, we all know that it happens without trying. It turns out that most of us have forgotten how to breathe deeply and, to compound the problem, poor posture, lots of sitting, sucking in our bellies, even wearing tight clothes, stops us from breathing well. In fact, it's believed that many of us are only using 70 per cent of our lung capacity with every breath due to shallow or inefficient breathing.

By practising diaphragmatic breathing, otherwise known as belly breathing, we can not only heal by lowering the amount of cortisol in our bodies (thereby levelling out moods, assisting with better sleep and improving our brains' abilities to focus and make decisions), but also lower both our blood pressure and heart rate. Over time, as we learn how to breathe to our full capacity and improve our posture, we also improve our core-muscle stability and reduce the chance of injury.

To practise is really simple and you can do it before you get out of bed in the morning or right before you go to sleep. It's best to begin practising when you're lying down, but once you get the hang of it, you'll be able to do it sitting or standing too.

Lie flat on your back and make sure you feel supported and comfortable—maybe that means you lie with your knees bent or cushions under your head. Place one hand on your upper chest and the other on your belly, just below your rib cage. Breathe in slowly through your nose, pulling the air deep into your lungs. As you do this, the hand on your chest should remain still, while the one on your belly should gently rise. Then, when your lungs are full of breath, tighten your abdominal muscles and draw them in towards your spine as you exhale slowly through your mouth. As you do this, the hand on your belly should return to its original position while the hand on your chest remains still. Repeat this ten times, as often as you remember to, during the day and pay attention to how you feel both during and after.

TAKE A NAP

Of course, there will be days (probably many of them) when the idea of a daytime nap feels ridiculous. Work is too busy, kids are too full-on, study is relentless and so on. On those days, finding time to steal away for an hour of shut-eye is just not on the cards. The good news is that neuroscientists now believe for most adults, the optimal nap length is closer to twenty minutes than an hour, and even as little as ten minutes of snoozing can have a positive impact on both our cognitive function and emotional regulation. A study by Janna Mantua and Rebecca Spencer published in the *Journal of Sleep Medicine* in 2017 found that napping can facilitate both cognitive and emotional health and 'the benefits are present even if a sufficient amount of sleep is obtained during the night prior'.

If you're exhausted and find yourself needing a brief siesta, find somewhere quiet to snooze (under your desk, in your car, under a tree in your backyard, on the lounge while your kids watch TV—and set your alarm for twenty minutes. This means you will wake up before your brain slips into the REM part of your sleep cycle, avoiding the groggy, cranky feeling that comes from being woken up out of deep sleep. It also means you will wake up feeling surprisingly refreshed. I know twenty minutes doesn't sound like very much time, but it can be the difference between finishing the day entirely depleted and finishing the day well.

RESTORATIVE YOGA

For soul-deep healing that's so easy you can do it in bed, try adding a basic restorative yoga pose or two to your day. While we've already looked at the evidence showing that regular yoga practice improves

Twenty minutes doesn't sound like very much time, but it can be the difference between finishing the day entirely depleted and finishing the day well.

our mental health, even adding a single stand-alone restorative pose to your night-time routine has shown enormous benefits to sleep, with a University of Mississippi study showing that yoga 'resulted in a significant decrease in the time taken to fall asleep, an increase in the total number of hours slept and in the feeling of being restored in the morning'.

One of my most enduring bedtime rituals involves a few minutes of legs up the wall pose and/or reclined bound angle pose. I suppose I'm cheating by admitting this, but I often do these while I'm reading in bed, and still find them incredibly relaxing.

A quick search will show you there are dozens of restorative poses to try at home, but here are three that anyone can try, and they can all be done in bed. (If you find any of these poses uncomfortable, look online for variations. By adding pillows or blankets you should be able to find a position that's not only comfortable, but also leaves you feeling totally supported.)

LEGS UP THE WALL

Exactly what it says on the box: in this pose you put your legs up the wall. I find it helpful to scoot my backside close to the wall first and then stretch my legs up one at a time, adjusting until the angle feels comfortable. Then simply lie still, breathe deeply (maybe even include some diaphragmatic breathing at the same time) and enjoy the weightless sensation of having your feet and legs inverted. This pose not only feels beautiful but also reduces our heart rate, which leads to a reduction in anxiety and insomnia.

RECLINED BOUND ANGLE POSE

This is another pose you can do lying on your back: simply bend your knees and place your feet together. Then gently allow your knees to fall out to each side, creating a diamond shape with your

soften your body

legs. Adding some deep breathing here is an option, as is supporting your knees or back with cushions or blankets. This pose has been found to improve circulation and reduce symptoms of stress.

CHILD'S POSE

One of the simplest poses in yoga, it is one of the most soothing and comforting too. Simply kneel on your bed (on the floor, a yoga mat, or wherever you feel comfortable), rest your backside on your heels, and soften your chest towards your thighs. If you can, rest your forehead on the floor and either stretch your hands up past your head, palms on the floor, or let them rest gently against your legs. Breathe and soften your body into the pose and let any tension seep out of you with each breath. Practising child's pose not only offers comfort and calms the mind, but it's also been shown to relieve fatigue and gently releases back and neck tension.

~~~~~~~~

JOURNALLING

As a healing tool, journalling is, to put it mildly, a surprise package. I've been an on-and-off journaller since I was an angsty teen and know from experience the singular clarity that writing out my feelings can bring. What I didn't know until recently is just how powerful a tool it really is.

There's been a surprising amount of research on the various benefits of journalling, which could fill an entire chapter on their own.

At a glance though, there's evidence that journalling:

- **helps reduce stress**
- improves our immune function (yes, really!)
- **boosts memory and comprehension**
- improves mood
- **provides a greater sense of overall wellbeing**
- offers emotional catharsis
- **helps regulate emotions**
- develops a greater sense of self-identity.

What's more, researchers at The University of Auckland discovered that writing by hand may help us to heal faster and sleep better, while an article published by the Association of Psychological Science found that writing by hand improves both comprehension and critical thinking.

Excitingly, for the time-poor among us, researchers have found that journalling doesn't need to happen daily to deliver us many of these benefits. A 2005 study published in *Advances in Psychiatric Treatment* showed just fifteen to twenty minutes of journalling, once or twice a month, can be enough to lower blood pressure and improve liver functionality. Alternatively, writing a single sentence every day can help develop more detailed, positive memories and make us happier.

A journal can look however you want—a cheap spiral-bound notebook you write one line in every day; a fancy, leather-bound book you add to once a month; or something in between. Regardless, it offers you an opportunity for both physical healing (the previously mentioned study from *Advances in Psychiatric Treatment* also showed that journallers have fewer doctors' appointments than non-journallers) as well as emotional healing. It gives us a tool for self-exploration and self-awareness, a place where we can muddle out problems and come to realisations and, over time, it can become another avenue for you to create a healthy relationship with yourself.

Please remember, as you begin to consider what healing might look like to you, that none of the suggestions in this chapter should feel heavy on your shoulders, and you don't need to do them out of obligation. They simply offer an opportunity for you to recognise (and act as though) you deserve to feel supported, grounded, rested, well and cared for.

IF YOU HAVE HALF A MINUTE

- Practise three rounds of diaphragmatic breathing.

- Jot down one sentence to sum up your day, or even a specific memory of that day.

- Take a big, juicy stretch—hands above your head or behind your back and feel some tension seep out of your shoulders and neck.

- Look at your schedule for the week ahead and choose one commitment to cancel or postpone.

- When someone asks you to do something, respond with, 'Let me get back to you,' then ask your inner rebel what to do.

- Begin your day by setting an intention: 'I will honour my boundaries today' or 'I'm allowed to say no'.

- Try a thirty-second mindfulness meditation by studying one of your five senses—what can I see, taste, hear, feel or smell?

IF YOU HAVE HALF AN HOUR

- Try a stream-of-consciousness journal entry, where you write whatever comes to your mind, with no censoring and no judgement.

- Take a nap.

- Talk to a friend about doing a weekly kid-swap or cooking a meal for each other once a fortnight.

- Take a yin yoga class (in person or online).
- Make an appointment with a psychologist or counsellor.
- Call a mental health hotline for a chat.
- Learn tai chi from YouTube.
- Call a friend or loved one and have a good cry.
- Write out your negative thoughts or resentments and burn the piece of paper, releasing them as they turn to ash.
- Follow a guided meditation (Insight Timer has lots of great, free options).
- Eat breakfast for dinner and, in the time you save, take a bath or sit outside with a drink.

IF YOU HAVE HALF A DAY OR MORE

- Create a retreat at home with yoga, meditation, journalling and a nourishing meal.
- Go to a museum or gallery and wander slowly, feeling your feelings and thinking your thoughts.
- Spend time among the trees and remember the healing they offer you.
- Cook up a big pot of delicious soup or stew and freeze it in batches—future you will be so grateful for the reprieve.
- Make a list of ideas from this book that feel healing to you, then do them, one at a time.

conclusion

I spend a lot of time thinking about the world.

How big and small it is. How much it can change and how much it stays the same. How you're reading this book in a different world from the one in which I wrote it, and how some things are powerful enough to pierce the divide between the two. I think that words are one. I think that care is another.

I've come to believe that care takes time and makes it *more*. Acts of care endure for far longer than the time it takes to do them, because they continue to exist as generosity, empathy, inspiration, awe and joy in hearts and minds. And I believe that's true no matter how seemingly insignificant the acts of care are. As we've discovered, these acts of Small Care are slow and sustainable, and incredibly powerful.

In spite of this, some people might see the ideas presented in this book as so simplistic, so everyday and accessible that there's no way they could possibly change the world. How can planting a seed or waving at a neighbour or lying in a park on your lunchbreak be powerful? All I can say is, try it and see.

We've looked at so many different ways Small Care can improve our physical and mental health, sleep, creativity, self-esteem, problem-solving abilities and critical-thinking skills. We saw how Small Care can provide us with heightened feelings of belonging, trust, empathy, generosity, respect, connection and intimacy, all of which have an undeniable impact on the way we live in the world— the way we relate to people, the way we listen and behave and show up for strangers and loved ones and places and ideas.

Just for a moment, I want you to imagine a scenario where you are experiencing some of these positive shifts in your own life. Improved health, a sense of belonging, heightened connection, kindness and compassion for people you know and those you don't, improvements in happiness and creativity and critical thinking and cognitive function. Now imagine what the flow-on effects of those improvements could be for you. What would be different if your sleep was better and your mental health improved, for example? Or how might you operate with bolstered self-esteem and strengthened problem-solving abilities? What difference would it make if you felt more generous and more connected to others? What shifts, what new perspectives and possibilities would these changes open up to you?

Now, imagine how the impact of those changes would be multiplied and amplified if everyone you met were to experience them. Think how far the benefits would spread as they fanned out into the world. Imagine more and more people feeling better, feeling elevated or loved or respected or seen or heard or connected or nurtured. Giving their time, offering their kindness, finding solutions and creating stronger bonds. At its most fundamental, this is how we change the world. This is Small Care, brought to life.

So where to from here? Now that we know care can come in so many forms, what does it look like to care more?

For me, today at least, care looks like a small spider named Fred. Fred lives in his silken castle in the corner of our bathroom window and was named by our son, who is feeding Fred flies to 'make sure he has enough to eat'. This somewhat disgusting act of love, of care, of connection, has sent waves through our family that I could never have expected. Last week, our daughter, who was positively *not* on Team Fred, came out of the bathroom with a big smile on her face and told me she'd watched Fred catch, kill and eat a fly. 'It was awesome, Mum,' she said. 'Pretty gross, but awesome.' (Team Fred has since expanded.) Then, just yesterday, our son overheard Ben's plan to de-cobweb the house over the weekend and made us promise not to move Fred. 'We can't kick him out of his house! Imagine if spiders kicked us out of our house?'

Fred has offered the four of us a tiny but potent shift in perspective in how we all—friends, strangers, mammals and arachnids alike— live in the same world, inhabit the same spaces, are part of the same complex web (ha!) of connection. Feeding, watching and caring for Fred led to a collective experience for our family, which led to a new connection with each other. It led to generosity, further kindnesses and a reminder that nature is everywhere.

Beyond that, it's hard to trace the effects that ripple out from Fred. We do know that connection to nature helps us to reduce stress, increase happiness and develop a sense of responsibility for the natural places we love, while experiencing awe results in a reduction in materialism, an increased sense of humility, a higher likelihood of giving our time and energy to others and an expanded perception of time. We know that kindness breeds kindness, not only for the person offering the kind turn but also those who observe it, and we know that the idle moments spent simply observing a spider build its web offer us a chance to recalibrate, to problem-solve and make new connections between seemingly disparate ideas. It's also an exercise in the healing art of mindfulness, which brings us perspective, contentment and gratitude. So, when you have a person or, in this case, four people who have benefited from those improvements, directly or indirectly, all of which stemmed from a tiny act of care shown to a spider, it becomes far easier to see just how big an impact Small Care can have in the world.

Today, care looks like Fred. On other days it might look like:

- receiving a box of oranges from our neighbours and making marmalade to share
- inviting our friend Will over for a game of backyard cricket
- chatting to Jan at the local coffee shop while we wait for our breakfast
- going for a mountain-bike ride and swimming in the waterhole at the end of the trail
- showing up to my psychologist appointment prepared to be honest and curious
- Zooming with mates overseas
- writing a poem for a friend and sending it to her in the mail
- working at our local community garden
- holding hands with Ben as we walk to the redwoods
- looking at photos of our trip up the Dempster Highway in the Yukon
- playing 'Truth Hurts' by Lizzo really loud (three times) to get me out of a bad mood.

Some of the ideas, both in this list and in earlier chapters, seem contradictory. Do I get off tech or do I look at photos of nature on my computer? Do I play with my kids or do I honour the healing I need and go for a walk alone? Do I enjoy the single-minded peace of making something or give my time to a community project? Well, the answer is: you can't do both. Not at the same time. Care will look different on different days, in different seasons of life, and there are options and ideas listed in this book to suit different situations. Over time and through experimentation, you can create your own beautiful, multifaceted kind of care.

Spend time outdoors with your family and play a game of soccer to find connection and movement, tap into nature and play. Join a pottery class and create a pinch pot for your mum in order to make, play, connect and practise kindness. Sit in a garden and watch the comings and goings of birds and insects to be idle, to heal, to show kindness to yourself and find awe in your natural neighbourhood.

There is no wrong way to care. Just throw that pebble and see what happens.

Ram Dass once wrote, 'We're all just walking each other home,' and while I think that's beautiful and true, I also think it's what we do on the way that matters.

You and I have explored hundreds of ideas that are powerful enough to change the world. Rest assured, no one person needs to shoulder the burden of doing it all by themselves, we only need to cast our eyes forward and start small, with care.

we're all just walking

each other home

To you,

Who is magnificent.

Your heart spools

its red threads into the world

and you let it—

even when it hurts—

because, my friend,

hearts bleed.

It's what they do.

Built for it,

they pump their bounty

into our limbs, our brains, our hands and faces

They spill their abundance

and the world blooms.

Hope blooms.

Love and joy and gentleness explode

in riotous colour,

enduring fireworks.

As you see the wild garden

unfurling before you,

its crimson vines rambling up walls,

flowers heavy with nectar and bees,

remember—

each red thread has two ends,

one that attaches it to the world,

the other

to your own dear heart.

about the author

Brooke McAlary loves words. Reading them, writing them, listening to them and playing around with them. So it's a fortunate thing that she became an author, because there's really no other job she feels qualified to do. She is the bestselling author of three non-fiction books, including *Destination Simple* and *Slow*. Brooke is also a tree-hugger, a mountain-lover, honorary Canadian (this is a made-up thing but she stands by it), moderately successful gardener, and the creator and co-host of the #1 Health show, The Slow Home Podcast, where she talks to interesting people about what it means to live slow in a fast-paced world.

She lives in the Southern Highlands of New South Wales with her husband Ben, two kids, two dogs, lots of fruit trees, many wild birds who eat the fruit of said fruit trees and a spider named Fred.

acknowledgements

Most writing is solitary, which means a writer needs to navigate the ups and downs and self-doubts on their own (or at least try to). Publishing a book, however, is a different beast altogether, and requires a team of collaborators to bring it into the world. I was lucky enough to have a wonderful team again for this book. To the crew at Allen & Unwin, including my publisher, Kelly Fagan; Angela Handley; Alice Grundy; Dannielle Viera; and designer Madeleine Kane—thank you all for helping make this book as good as it could be. To the sales, marketing, production and distribution teams, thank you for getting *Care* and her message out into the world. To my agent, Grace Heifetz, thank you for listening to me talk about all the ways in which 2020 was a rough year (and also the perfect year) to write about hope and time. To dear Katey Hawley, illustrator and miracle-worker, thank you for putting your heart on the page alongside mine. I'm forever grateful to all of you.

To friends and family who listened, encouraged and comforted me at various points, thank you for caring in all the many ways that care exists. Isla and Toby, thank you for being your kind, awe-filled, playful selves. The world is in good hands with you two. To Ben, for the space and support and Moonacres' broccoli sandwiches, for thick and thin and everything in between, thank you. I love you, and I like you.

P.S. I have created a full list of articles, studies, links and helpful resources over on my website. Head over to slowyourhome.com/careresources to dig a little deeper.

First published in 2021

Copyright © Brooke McAlary 2021

Allen & Unwin
83 Alexander Street
Crows Nest NSW 2065
Australia
Phone: (61 2) 8425 0100
Email: info@allenandunwin.com
Web: www.allenandunwin.com

A catalogue record for this
book is available from the
National Library of Australia

ISBN 978 1 76087 820 7

Internal design by Madeleine Kane
Illustrations by Katey Hawley
Printed by C&C Offset Printing Co. Ltd, China

10 9 8 7 6 5 4 3 2 1